Cory is one of the m… …en that I know. His experience performing … the NFL informs his philosophy on big time financial decisions. This book encourages readers to lead their wealth with clarity and conviction.

Matt Pittman | CEO, Meat Church

Cory Procter brings the mindset of a professional athlete and the discipline of a seasoned wealth strategist to this powerful guide. *Built Not Broke* reframes wealth as something to protect, grow, and steward with intention.

Casey Donahew | Country Musician, Entrepreneur

As someone who built a restaurant empire from the ground up – risking everything to make it happen – I know what it means to protect what you built. Cory Procter gets it. *Built Not Broke* is the financial playbook every entrepreneur needs.

Marty Bryan | Founder & Owner, Marty B's Ventures & Circle Star Brands

This is not about chasing returns. It is about building something durable. Cory equips business owners with the mindset and structure to safeguard what they have built.

Alex Melen | Co-Founder, SmartSites

Cory Procter brings integrity and insight to the conversation about wealth. His philosophy centers on stewardship, preparation, and purposeful growth.

Tamara Nall | CEO & Founder, *The Leading Niche*

The emphasis on resilience distinguishes this book from typical financial guides. Cory demonstrates how to design systems that withstand pressure and protect families for generations.

Shawn Johal | Business Growth Coach, Elevation Leaders, Bestselling Author of *The Happy Leader*

This is a strategic resource for entrepreneurs with significant assets who want to move from accumulation to protection and legacy. Cory analyzes investments from multiple perspectives and presents clear direction.

Takehito Yokoo | CEO, Jozen Power LLC

A thoughtful perspective on what it means to build financial strength. Cory emphasizes resilience, protection, and long-term discipline over short-term gains.

Aaron Poynton | Bestselling Author,
Think Like A Black Sheep

Built Not Broke delivers a clear, disciplined approach to wealth, rooted in experience and focused on protection, purpose, and long-term impact. It brings much-needed clarity to the decisions that matter most when the stakes are high.

Carl Grant III | Author of *How to Live the Abundant Life*

A compelling reminder that durable wealth is built through intentional decisions, not chance. Cory provides structure for navigating financial transitions with confidence.

Dr. Rahul R. Prasad | Best-selling author of *Impact Shift and Success DNA*, physicist, philanthropist, and investor

BUILT
NOT
BROKE

THE PURSUIT OF RESILIENT WEALTH

BY CORY PROCTER

ISBN **979-8-9939186-1-7** (pbk)
ISBN **979-8-9939186-0-0** (ebook)
ISBN **979-8-9939186-2-4** (hcv)

Library of Congress Control Number: **2026907113**

DEDICATION

To my Lord, Jesus Christ, for giving me the test that became a testimony. For giving me a faith that is firm and gives more meaning and depth than this life ever could.

To my wife, Megan, for being a leader in our home. For taking the first step in our faith. For dealing with my intensity and bringing peace to our lives. For choosing to love me.

To my children—Grace, Hank, and Faith—you bring me so much joy just to be with you. Grace, with your snuggles. Hank, with your wrestling. Faith, with your kisses and love. Daddy loves you so much.

To my parents, for instilling a work ethic that is unrivaled. For doing everything you could with what you had. For holding me accountable as a kid and as an adult. Much of my work was built on top of a foundation you have set. I love you.

To my nephew, Evan, who was a catalyst of my faith. From pain and anger to a vision and purpose. You are Big E. You're the reason I call Grace and Faith "Honey." You took care of that. I'll never stop because of your choice. Give all the pups a treat and pound from us.

To the coaches and teachers who helped develop me in the formative years and beyond. You were a bigger part of my life. Coach Ancira, for talking me through hard times. Coach McKinney, for calling me out early. Coach McKay, for bringing me into your family. Coach Germer, for being the real deal. To all the teachers that saw more in me than I could. It takes a village, and I needed you.

To everyone who has trusted and had faith in me—family, friends, employees, colleagues, and clients. You know who you are. It takes a team to do what we do. I'll never forget the ones who stood with me in the fire.

ACKNOWLEDGMENTS

Special thanks to my writing coach and mentor, Phoenix Roberts, without whom this book couldn't have been completed.

Thank you to Erin Botsford for being a huge coach and mentor in the financial space, and for bringing wisdom and a bigger vision to my business.

Thank you to my mastermind group for pushing me to take the risk to write this book. Fedro, Kono, Wheeler, Jeppson, and Cotton. I don't care what anyone says about you. You're OK in my book!

Thank you to Chad Willardson and his team at Platinum Elevated. What a great group of people forcing growth. Proximity is power.

To my accountability coach, Trav, for helping me get home on my weight and nutrition, and for family and business accountability. You don't go through the things and conversations we've been through without becoming mates.

Thank you to the men in my life for keeping my feet to the fire in my faith, family, and business.

Table of Contents

Introduction

Trust

In any professional relationship, trust is vital. Why should you trust me with your money? There are two reasons—lessons I learned early in life:

First, if we're smart, we learn from our mistakes. If we're very smart, we learn from others' mistakes and don't repeat them.

Second, I've been where you are now, wondering if what I built will last.

Saying this might look a little weird right out of the gate, mainly because I always hate it when anyone says "trust me" after I ask a question. When someone says, "Trust me," my natural response is, "That's for me to decide."

I know that trust has its limits. The people I trust with my kids may not be the same people I trust with my money. I may, based on our shared history, trust someone completely in one category while needing to create a shared history in another area to build trust there. So I will share my story and how we dealt with the problems that arose, and you can decide for yourself.

Very Short Stories

In high school, I got into a car accident. I rear-ended a lady and she filed a lawsuit against us. A year later, my mom and stepdad filed for bankruptcy–lost their home, car, and a lot more–because of that suit.

My father was a veterinarian; specifically, he treated thoroughbred horses. You'd think he'd get wealthy working in such a high-class industry, but that's not always the case. Breeding horses is a high-overhead business, and owning your own medical practice (in any branch of medicine) is costly. Some doctors do get rich, while many live comfortable, but not lavish, lifestyles. My mother contributed, working up to three jobs at a time, to make our family finances work.

Then came the divorces–both my parents, both more than once, all of them were a big hit to the wallet.

I've lived through my family's issues and money was always part of those issues. I've seen them in others and I've trained myself to know how to protect **my money**. What I do to protect mine is what led me to help others like you.

The Lessons

When I got the dream call and signed a contract to play in the National Football League (NFL), I wasn't worried about the guy who'd promise me an extra point or two in my port-folio. I was worried about not screwing it up on the field! This wasn't just my dream, it was my job and, for most players, it's a job that doesn't last long. In finance, it's pretty much the same. Lots of people who get a chance to make a lot of money very quickly end up losing it because they screw it up. They aren't trained to survive the inevitable hard times, so when those times come, the money goes.

From Mom and Dad

Dad the Vet was at the track on weekends or, pretty much, whenever we visited. During foaling season, he had to deliver that foal at any time of the day or night, and maybe several on the same night. During racing season, the horses, who are athletes, had to be watched for injuries, diet, and anything else that could affect their performance. If they got injured, the injury had to be mended and the animal rehabilitated. None of this stops during the off-season. There was a little less time pressure, but you still had to watch their diet, watch out for injuries, and much more in order to keep them in top (money-making) form.

Dad often said that he had no problem making money; holding on to it was another matter altogether. He had to pay for supplies, equipment, insurance, travel, everything. He billed his clients for everything, but those expenses still took a big portion of his gross income.

Meanwhile, mom did what she had to do to make ends meet. (Very cliché, but we repeat clichés because they remain true.) I saw all this as a kid and just naturally developed a frugal mindset:

If I spent it, it was gone, and I'd need to work to replace it.

In the NFL

One website estimated that over a million boys played high school football during the 2022-23 season.[1] The NFL rosters

---

[1] Jeff Fisher, "High School Football Participation Moves Back Above 1-Million Players," *HighSchoolFootballAmerica.com*, 13 September 2023. https://highschoolfootballamerica.com/high-school-football-participation-grows-above-1-million-players

total about 1,700 players.[2] The average professional football career lasts less than three and a half years.[3]

Even though I didn't know those numbers back then, from the start, I knew I was lucky to be in the draft. When that was over, I was less lucky. I was a "free agent"—no team thought I was good enough for the big call up or the big money. I did get hired to join the practice squad, but that group generally didn't last more than a year or two. I lasted six because I got called up to the main roster, even started in a few games, and loved every minute of it. I was never Pro Bowl material, but I was smart. In fact, Bill Parcells (head coach of the Dallas Cowboys from 2003 to 2006) complimented me by saying, "Grizz, you're pretty smart. You're no genius, but you're pretty smart."

I was just smart enough to know that I wasn't the best player on the team, but I could be the guy that was willing to do the work and do it right.

So I learned to be the guy that showed up when and where I needed to be. I learned the rules and my playbook. I asked good questions so I didn't make devastating mistakes or become a massive liability in the games I played.

---

[2] Unbylined, "How Many Active NFL Players Are There?" *BetMGM.com*, 12 September 2024. https://sports.betmgm.com/en/blog/nfl/how-many-active-nfl-players-are-there-bm25/#:~:text=There%20are%201%2C696%20active%20players%20in%20the%20NFL

[3] John Keim, "With average NFL career 3.3 years, players motivated to complete MBA program," *ESPN.com*, 29 July 2016. https://www.espn.com/blog/nflnation/post/_/id/207780/current-and-former-nfl-players-in-the-drivers-seat-after-completing-mba-program

That's why the guy who should've lasted just one or two seasons lasted six and would've lasted a few more without that career-ending injury.

As a "Former"

Most of that first year after my knee blew up, I spent on the couch. That generally sucked but, in 2011, I married my smokin' hot wife, Megan. Even though I literally limped down the aisle, I fully expected to recover enough to get back with a team.

It didn't happen. I tried to rehab and had five surgeries, but the knee never fully recovered. We lived in New Jersey while I was trying to get back up to speed. I got to the point where I was sick of waiting for a coach, an agent, a scout, or somebody else to call me in. I remember looking at Megan and saying, "Babe, we've got to start making choices for ourselves." In March 2013, we moved to Texas and bought a home, still holding out for somebody to call me. It still didn't happen. I remember sitting there, cussing at my agent, watching slop on the field, and feeling like I was much better than many of them.

In Texas, I refused to simply sit on the couch. I completed a degree in psychology from the University of Montana (Go Griz!) and started working on my post-football issues, which were many. Fortunately, I got one last chance, I went to New Orleans for their rookie minicamp. (Our union's collective bargaining agreement at that time allowed this to happen.)

It was cool because I had a good time there, even though it was "no pads," meaning we didn't really play as hard as we could've. I was, honestly, relaxed enough that I was thinking, "I'm not going to be so uptight or intense. I'm just gonna go play, be cool with the coaches, say thank you for the opportunity, and do my best."

Sean Payton was there, and he was great with me. In fact, all the coaches were telling me, "You're exactly what we're looking for, but we're gonna look at these young guys." That was the smart move on their part. As a six-year veteran, my contract would've been more expensive. I was older and had a bunch of surgeries. They had younger, healthier, cheaper guys ready to play–guys they could develop over the next several years–whereas I'd already outlived the average NFL career by almost double. They were all super gracious, which gave me the kind of closure that my head needed to be sure my football days were done.

The realities (the hard times) of the game sank in. It was, "Been there, done that, got the T-shirt" for me.

The life I dreamed of, the win I earned, the income that I never had before (and most people never do) was suddenly gone because of something I couldn't control.

So I did what I'd always done: I got back up and went back to work. I channeled my competitive drive into sales, joining a start-up beverage company out of Atlanta. We hit it off, and over the next four years, I earned a couple promotions and a lot of valuable lessons before life called me in a new direction.

At the time, I didn't know if that company would be my forever home. After football, I just needed something to pour myself into while I figured out what came next. So I picked a new direction, started walking, and trusted that if it wasn't right, God would show me another way.

As a Money Manager

Risk Management

Those are the most important words in this book. Keep those two words in mind as we go through this journey together.

With all new clients, we talk about risk management at our first meeting. We describe some of the train wrecks (situations that arise which can destroy your financial security) and how we can take care of the important people in our lives should those disasters strike.

I'm not here to disparage my fellow financial planning professionals. Most are very good at what they do. I think, however, most weren't trained to see the whole picture. They're in business to make money–for you and for them. Mostly, we make money through AUM (assets under management), meaning how much of your money we oversee. Too many of them get focused on AUM and forget the other side of the coin.

If a disaster arises and your portfolio tanks, they have less AUM to manage and you have less money working for you.

You both lose.

At Pro Capital Wealth Management, rule number one is: *don't lose it*. Rule number two is: *make it work for you*. You might think number two should be number one, but your money can't work for you if you lose it. Protecting what you have, so that it can work for you, should always be your priority.

Control

We had a nice nest egg from my NFL paychecks, but it was in the hands of other people. That is, I had financial advisors telling me what I should do. That didn't satisfy me. I'd been in situations where other people were in control of my life; they made the decisions, and I went where I was told and did as I was told. I was interested in and aware of my investment portfolio during my playing days and after, but now I decided to take full control of my finances.

No one has a bigger interest in your success than you.

Here's a hard truth: your advisor might like you, but you're not their lifeline. If your finances crash, their business keeps running. They'll find new clients and keep playing the game.

That hit me. No one was coming to save me. So I chose to take control and become a wealth manager myself.

If that's not your path, that's fine, but you better have a game plan. Find an advisor you can trust, someone who knows the risk you took as an entrepreneur and fights for your financial life like it's their own. Because in this game, you can't afford to hand the ball to someone who doesn't care if you lose.

My advisor back then actually encouraged me to get a solid understanding of how my portfolio was developing, then encouraged me to branch out into my own business. I've always been a jump-in-headfirst instead of a toe-in-the-water kind of guy, so it took me a while to figure out how I wanted to make all this happen. When the path became clear to me, I ran down that path as fast as my aging knees could carry me.

I got the training and the licensing, and, in 2018, launched Pro Capital Wealth Management. Because I knew enough to know that I didn't know enough to succeed; it took a lot of work and I did that work. We were able to hit the ground running.

As an independent advisor, my team uses strategies that we know are effective for a specific type of client. We understand that how we work isn't right (meaning effective) for everyone, so we specialize. You'd think I'd go after athletes because I was one, and I have a couple of athletes as clients. Mostly, however, I deal with entrepreneurs, especially those with families. A person with a spouse and children is typically more risk-averse than one flying solo.

A pastor of my acquaintance once told me that guys work like trucks: they work better with a load. If a man has responsibilities, he's not so daring that he doesn't pay attention to the details. He's not so selfish that he just watches out for himself. He takes care of his people; there's a sense of responsibility that flows from our families to our other associations. It overshadows and overcomes our natural selfish nature. (Women are less prone to that selfishness, but it's in them as well, and they need to watch out for its quietly destructive effects.)

And, by the way, most entrepreneurs I've come in contact with are people from whom I've gained wisdom. They appreciate what others have built. They appreciate the effort their team puts into a project. They gain understanding from their work and they share that understanding freely. They're the kind of people that I think I relate to the most.

Entrepreneurs differ from what I'll call "paycheck men," which also includes women. A paycheck man with a problem calls HR, engineering, marketing, or research. An entrepreneur with a problem (often also a small business owner) knows he has no one to call. He understands it's on him to find the fix.

Many entrepreneurs, especially solopreneurs, feel a need to fix everything personally. Most of them get advice on how to do it, but they prefer to handle it themselves because they take their responsibilities very personally. The paycheck man shifts responsibility to HR, research, or somebody else.

I believe the most successful entrepreneurs (this goes for non-entrepreneurs, too) always hold on to the responsibility ("The Buck Stops Here," as President Harry Truman used to say), but they're willing to delegate technical problems to technical experts. Where their money is concerned, I'm a technical expert; I know what can and cannot be done. That's the mindset I want to work with.

(By the way, that's the reason I hired a great writing coach to make this book happen. I knew my story and I knew I needed help to get that story organized, polished, and make it flow smoothly. I am one hundred percent onboard with hiring anybody who has an ability that I don't have.)

Like my NFL goal, my financial management goal is simple: I want to leave a legacy for my children's children. I want to do awesome things while being sure I take care of those I love. As an NFL offensive lineman, I was there to protect the quarterback. As your financial management partner, I'm here to help you protect your assets as zealously as I protect my own.

So, let's get to it!

(Disclaimer: The stories you're about to read are true. The names and a few details have been altered to protect the privacy of those involved. Some accounts are composites of several individuals. Any similarity to actual persons is coincidental.)

Part I
The Foundation

Why Successful People End Up Broke

Preface

For the record, I am a licensed and experienced financial planner. I've spent years learning everything I can about ways to grow and protect wealth. I did it with mine and started the business to do it for others. Even so, I don't know everything–I'm still learning. This book was written to point out some of the questions you ought to be asking so that you could be an active participant in planning your financial future.

That said, some disclaimers are necessary:

Every single person's situation is different–even if you're husband and wife.

Every person's situation changes over time. (Remember that; we'll come back to it often!)

Unless you are my client and we have a signed agreement to that effect, this book is **not** financial planning advice from me for you. This book is solely and entirely general information presented to help you understand the need for financial planning and to outline a few basic ideas so that you can have an intelligent conversation with **your** financial planner.

I wish you the best in whatever you do, and I hope I've given you a lot of things to think about.

So let's huddle up!

To ensure compliance with requirements imposed by the IRS under Circular 230, we inform you that any US Federal tax advice contained in this communication, unless otherwise specifically stated, was not intended or written to be used, and cannot be used, for the purpose of (1) avoiding penalties under the Internal Revenue Code or (2) promoting, marketing, or recommending to another party any matters addressed herein.

Any investments or strategies referenced herein do not take into account the investment objectives, financial situation, or particular needs of any specific person. Product suitability must be independently determined for each individual investor. Pro Capital LLC explicitly disclaims any responsibility for product suitability or suitability determinations related to individual investors.

Some investments or products mentioned herein may be considered complex investment products. Such products contain unique risks, terms, conditions, and fees specific to each offering. Depending upon the particular product, risks include, but are not limited to, issuer credit risk, liquidity risk, market risk, the performance of an underlying derivative financial instrument, formula, or strategy. Return of principal is not guaranteed above FDIC insurance limits or may be subject to the creditworthiness of the issuer. You should not purchase an investment product or make an investment until you have read the specific offering documentation and understand the specific investment terms and risks of such investment.

Any guarantees or benefits provided by insurance are subject to the claims paying ability of the issuing insurance company.

CHAPTER 1

The Wake-Up Calls

Fundamental Ideas:

1. For every action, there are consequences, and some of them are harsh.
2. What you don't know can destroy you.
3. The greatest lesson you can learn is how much you don't know.

It Started with an Accident

One day, during the summer before my senior year of high school, I went with my younger brother, Casey, to lift weights at the high school with our football team. On the way, I dozed off for just a second or two. Casey yelled at me when a woman stopped to turn into her apartment complex. I hit the brakes, but it wasn't enough to avoid her altogether. We didn't hit full-on, but it was enough.

So we pulled into the apartment complex, and she ran off without saying a word to us. I assumed she was calling the police. When she came back out a few minutes later, we made sure nobody was hurt, and we waited.

Of course, I called my mom while the woman was in her apartment. She and my stepdad, Charlie, showed up a few minutes later. The police then arrived and wrote up a report, even though formal reports really aren't needed when nobody's hurt. They did their thing, and then we all went our separate ways.

I remember my stepdad really stood up and took care of everything. Unfortunately, that turned out to be a lot. This was what our insurance company called a "second fault." I'd gotten a speeding ticket a few weeks earlier for going about 35 in a 25 zone. Ironically, the warning letter arrived the same day as my accident, stating that if I had one more infraction, they were going to kick me off the insurance policy.

More than anything else about that accident, I remember sitting there while waiting for everyone to arrive, thinking the lady I just rear-ended was fine. Maybe it was a moment of typical teen denial. I don't remember her being distraught or anything but in spite of the fact that she appeared to be just fine, she filed a lawsuit. I remember mom and Charlie telling me about it, though they didn't say much—just, "Well, we've got a lawsuit right now because of this lady." Mom was never one to share much about money. She didn't hide it from me; she just thought that money was their business and not something you talked about with kids.

I did learn that the woman was a dog groomer, and that became a major point of contention. Mom and Charlie were thinking, "What are you talking about? She's a dog groomer. She's not making that much money. She's not doing that much. This doesn't really qualify as a major issue," or something like that.

Eventually, they shared a few bits of the story. An investigator did check the woman out. She was grooming large-breed dogs, and, for some reason I never learned, she couldn't work, so she received payments for damages and lost wages.

I never found out what kind of number that settlement included, nor did I ever know what kind of financial position my mom and stepdad were in because they were so private about that stuff. (On another occasion, I remember passing the desk and seeing a check for something like $3,000. I thought, "We're rich!" like any kid would do, but mom grabbed the check and said, "That's none of your business," and I thought, "Okay, I'm keeping out of their business.")

Being a teen, I was more focused on myself than anything else. Of course, I felt horrible because Mom and Charlie were very disappointed in me. I got kicked off the insurance and rode the bus to and from school during my senior year. I had to walk maybe a quarter mile to the street where the bus stopped every day, then walk back home after school.

It wasn't until I came home for Christmas break during my freshman year of college that I saw the effects of that day. Mom, Charlie, and Casey had moved to an apartment. I found out they had to file bankruptcy because of the settlement and somehow lost the house. It was weird to see. It was a great house. Even so—and you'll excuse me for using an old cliché—that day changed all our lives.

A Little More Background

I'm the second of three boys (Clay, me, and Casey) from a second marriage for both my parents. When I was fairly young, they divorced. Mom and Charlie both remarried for a third go-round. My biological dad will tell you that his divorces really tore apart his net worth. Mom never even said that much. I never remember us being anything like a wealthy family, but we weren't poor by any stretch.

When mom married Charlie, he and his three kids (two girls and a boy) moved in with us. I slept on an air mattress for one summer until they bought a larger home. That meant six children under the same roof, sharing one bathroom. The boys all lived in the basement, unfinished at that time. A second bathroom came later on, but until then, I tried to get up earlier than the others to take a shower. That worked, to a point, but there was a lot of fighting among the siblings until we trickled, one by one, out of the house.

My older brother, Clay, had a kid fairly young. He moved out, started a family, and went to work. I went to college at the University of Montana and started my path. My younger brother, Casey, was the last one to stay before he went to trade school. As for my step-siblings, they all left home early for various reasons. We don't need to get into all the weird details; let's just say that we were far from the model family of Gig Harbor, Washington (a small town near the south end of Puget Sound). I have to admit there are a few "white trash" aspects to my family history. I always quip, "I can party white trash, I just don't want to *be* white trash."

So, maybe I shouldn't have been surprised to find the house gone and Mom, Charlie, and Casey in an apartment that I'd never heard anything about while at school. Nor should I have been surprised that my mom kind of downplayed it all.

"We just moved, you know. We just didn't need that big house anymore."

Casey told me, later, that they'd filed for bankruptcy. The bank actually repossessed the Suburban I got into the wreck with. It was a bad situation all around. I was embarrassed by the fact that I caused this big financial problem. If you're reading this, Mom, I'm sorry for it and thankful you showed strength to protect us from any undue pressure.

I should also mention that my parents' divorce decree included my brothers and me living with both Dad and Mom, six months at a time. That involved a lot of moving, as you'd guess, and was a disruptive cycle in our growing up. Even so, I appreciate all the things my parents did for us, more so now that I'm older and have children of my own.

For example, one time, I remember Mom giving me ten dollars, which became one of my first big financial lessons. A friend of mine got very excited, "Like, dude, you got ten bucks, let's go get some candy!" I decided I didn't want to get the candy. Even though I was a fat kid, I realized that if I spent the money, it would go away. Seeing the way my parents lived had made me super frugal or maybe instilled in me this healthy fear that if I spent it, it was gone. That lesson was compounded, I think, after the wreck and seeing what followed. In fact, when I got into the NFL to play ball, my first check from the Detroit Lions was an $8,000 signing bonus. Although that's not a ton of money, I looked at it and said to myself, "I don't want to touch this thing." Since then, out of every dollar I've earned, I've tried to keep as much as possible.

The Franchise Deal That Wasn't

After dealing with the consequences of my actions (both the good and the bad), I started seeing what could destroy money if you didn't take an active role in it.

When I was in the NFL, a teammate we'll call *Bob* signed one of the richest contracts in franchise history. He invested $12 million to buy a burger franchise for somewhere around thirty locations. Think about that–more money than most people make in a lifetime right out of the gate, just to get the rights to open fast-food restaurants in all those locations. He'd also committed himself to spending more to build the stores, staff them, advertise them, and whatever else he would've needed to do to make them successful (assuming, of course, that they were successful).

Well, they weren't. Again, no details needed beyond saying that he lost every penny of his investment. Another friend of mine went into this deal as a junior partner with Bob. He only put in around $200,000 and, luckily, got out before it all went to hell, but he still lost $10,000 or $20,000 in the deal.

I remember, after the fact, talking to Bob, asking, "Man, have you ever even worked in a restaurant?"

"No."

I said, "I mean, wouldn't you rather have tried one restaurant first before you signed up for, like, thirty of these things?"

Bob later found out that his advisor hadn't provided information to the SEC, as required by law. He sued that guy, who ended up getting barred because of it. I think that guy now sells insurance.

An Epiphany?

I'd like to say that, at some point, I had a great flash of inspiration or insight, a vision or whatever, but I didn't.

What I had instead was a slow burn. Seeing what I saw growing up certainly shaped me, but the realization that money has to be proactively managed came much later, and through experience more than epiphany. Let's face it, high school kids aren't exactly the target market for financial planning services.

I started to get a clue watching the franchise fiasco. I'd never had money like that, hadn't ever even seen it—and I definitely hadn't seen it disappear like that.

During my football years, I saw so many bad choices about money that I could fill a book with them. At the same time, life kept shifting. My career ended sooner than I had planned. I got married. Then we learned my one-year-old nephew had brain cancer, and soon we watched him go. Our first daughter was born during that fight.

Some of those moments I had control over; others, I had none at all. But all of them left a mark.

And while I wouldn't have called it a vision at the time, those experiences were stacking, preparing me for one.

Because one day, I finally had it.

We were invited to Milestone Church in Keller, Texas. I walked in hard-headed and proud, ready to challenge everything. But during worship, something shifted. I ran straight into a vision—one that broke the wall I'd built around myself. It was as if God took years of lessons, pain, and success, and pulled them together in that single moment.

That was when my life began to change. My faith grew. And that slow burn I'd been walking through became a fire, one that gave purpose to my money, my work, and my calling. That's when opportunities started coming my way.

Among them, I started looking at my whole history and saw a pattern. I started asking God, "Why are these I-have-no-control moments a repetitive thing in my life?" I asked a serious question and I got a serious answer, "Remember the wreck?"

I remembered my family losing everything because of an incident that initially lasted just a few seconds but had repercussions that have lasted to the present. I remembered the injury and the years it took my family to recover. I remembered losing a nephew and gaining a daughter—great pain mixed with absolute joy.

That's when it finally sank in: if I made a really bad choice, even unintentionally, I could make a choice so bad that it completely wrecked my finances or altered the whole trajectory of my life. Others also made choices, and some could affect my life so overwhelmingly that I might not recognize it as my life. A question naturally followed: how do I protect those I love?

All of a sudden, the pieces came together in the realization that, where money is concerned, I had no idea what I was doing. That's what I needed to fix.

I had developed what I initially called a healthy fear of financial disaster. When I came to fully understand that need, I decided I would never again be one disaster away from losing everything.

CHAPTER 2

What the NFL Taught Me about Money—and What It Didn't

Watch What Happens Around You, You'll Be Amazed at What You Learn

Fundamental Ideas:

1. Everybody makes mistakes, mostly because we never learned the right way to do it.
2. Someone is always eager to take advantage of you.
3. Where there is a lack of discipline, there is a lack of success.

Making It Into the Big League

What the public saw of my NFL career was a six-year joyride from the Detroit Lions to the Dallas Cowboys to the Miami Dolphins, complete with giant stadiums, cheering crowds, and great paychecks.

We (players and coaches) saw that too, and we loved it. If we paid attention, we also saw avoidable financial disasters.

I saw bad decisions from day one. Comerica Bank, headquartered in Detroit at that time, was a major Lions sponsor. They put an ATM in the facility, and we had a group of guys who would throw dice every day, all day long, in the locker room. Remember, my signing bonus was $8,000. The practice team rate was $60,000 a year in 2005–more money than I'd ever had before.

So, you can imagine the look on my face when I saw guys maxing out that ATM, bringing tens of thousands of dollars to the locker room to gamble. I mean, it was wild to see how much cash would be sitting there, and them betting like crazy–day after day!

After eleven games (out of the sixteen we had played each season back then), I signed with the Cowboys for those last few weeks. I'm focusing my story on my time with the Cowboys because I played most of my career with them and they're among the most famous NFL teams. Bob, the franchise wizard I mentioned before, was on that team and I worked with him and others long enough to see the effects of some of those bad decisions.

I didn't get on the field that first season, but I traveled with the team when we went to Las Vegas. I watched guys go down $10,000 or $20,000 at a table. That was their money and their business, but I saw that it as all about emotion. They desperately wanted to win it all back. So I saw some of them pull out a stack of hundred-dollar bills–$10,000 or whatever they'd lost–lay it down, and try to win it all back in one hand.

Yeah, that never happens.

I'm watching all this go by and thinking that this wasn't my natural behavior with money, especially with my history. I thought, but never said, "You guys are being completely reckless. Consider your losses as having had a good time, and don't get so emotional about it." I think that was what I saw everybody doing—making emotional choices. When you get emotional about money, you get to the point (very quickly) where you can destroy yourself financially. It was absolutely ludicrous and really sad.

I'm not going to say that what I saw—men just gambling their livelihoods away—I saw because they didn't want the money. That would've been too insane to believe, but that's what it looked like.

Craziest thing in the world.

Rookie Mistakes

One day, some years ago, I was on the phone with a player's dad, who told me how much his kid needed money. He didn't have money to pay his rent for the following month. He didn't have money to pay his baby mama for the next month. This is why I moved away from financial planning for professional athletes. At first, I went after them, until I saw how foolishly so many acted over money. I still have a couple of athlete clients but by and large, "utterly reckless" could be the nicest thing I can say about many of them. Some spend money on a completely emotional basis. I can't help them; planning takes logic and common sense, and some of those guys had none.

The First Fine

"Max" was a new receiver the year I was a rookie. He arrived late to our first team meeting ever. He had a huge contract before a new players' union collective bargaining agreement (CBA) put caps on rookie contracts, and he was late to the first meeting! I remember Steve Mariucci (Lions head coach that year) telling him, "We waited to start the meeting," and he didn't say it in a complimentary way. Why was Max late? Because he was buying a multimillion-dollar home, and that day was his closing. In high school, you probably remember, the coach made you run laps or something equally annoying. Coach Mariucci said, "I'm not going to run you; we just fine you in the NFL. We take your money. You're a big boy—act like a big boy." I was flabbergasted when I found out that fine was $30,000!

Max was always a good guy, but I could tell he wasn't going to make it. He came to training camp overweight. Anyone who knows physical fitness knows that it's a year-round thing. You can be in perfect shape on Super Bowl Sunday but if you don't lift weights, run, and generally keep active, you're flabby when training camp starts up in July. He was fined repeatedly for continually being overweight and late to meetings and when it all totaled up, the fines about equaled his whole rookie salary for the year—$230,000!

(By the way, as far as the IRS is concerned, he earned that money. The fact that he didn't collect it didn't bother them at all; they were happy to send out the tax bill anyway.)

I watched this happen in real time, all the while thinking, "I don't care how much money you have; to let money walk out the door like that is nuts."

The Truck and the Other Stuff

Everybody has situations. We're human, we make mistakes. I was introduced to a player with the Dallas Cowboys that needed help. When we met, I started asking questions about his situation. He had bought a $200,000 armored truck. You might call that a one-time purchase but there were other issues. He had a about $2 million in the bank and had been giving large chunks of cash to his girlfriend and mom for various reasons. There was a bigger issue in his attitude. He was lazy in his speech, his posture was one that he obviously didn't want to be there, and he even laid down on the couch in the office we were meeting at. He had a horrible attitude but I had given my word to people around him that I would meet with him.

"Number one," I told him, "you'll have to file a form 705 with the IRS for the money you're giving to your girlfriend and your mom. Those are gifts that are larger than our exemption rate, so you have to complete the right tax paperwork for them or you're getting a bill that you really won't like. Number two, what kind of insurance do you have on that armored truck?

"Look, people know where the players park. They will literally sit outside the facility to target you. Not all of them want an autograph. They want your money. You become a bigger target with money in the bank and a nice truck. It's public knowledge how much athletes get paid (which is dumb) and people come out of the woodwork to get a piece of it. What happens if you get in a car accident right out in front of the facility here, and that person wants to sue?"

He was arrogant. "I'll never give anybody that money."

"You can say that all you want, but the judge will tell you differently."

His response floored me. "I'll kill somebody before I give anybody my money."

"Okay, so you'll go broke AND go to jail. Great thinking."

To say the least, I could help, but the guy didn't want it. Frankly, I don't want those people as clients. They torpedo their own lives and blame everyone else in the process.

The Cowboys have invited me to talk to the rookies every year for most of a decade. I don't go to those meetings to talk football; I'm there to talk money. Where one guy wasn't listening, another player will. You can tell the guys who are listening. One first-round pick from last year came to the meeting with a perfect attitude: he was front and center, notepad on the desk, pencil in hand, alert, and when it came to my Q&A, he asked intelligent questions, like, "Where's a good place to start?"

I liked this guy immediately. He had something there and I'll bet he does the same in meetings for upcoming games. He'll have a career in pro football, and as of this writing, he's been off to a great start. This just goes to show, your attitude will absolutely determine your altitude.

The Lottery

You hear stories from other teams as well, but one of my teammates shared a story about how a guy went to a strip club and ended up getting one of the dancers pregnant. The player had a large contract at the time, so they nick-named the stripper "Jackpot" for winning the lottery and getting herself a baby daddy. I can't speak to the intentions of that specific girl, but I have been around long enough to know there are some bad ladies out there, too. Not every-one who makes you feel good has good intentions for you. Be careful where you hang out and whom you hang with.

The Entourage Effect

When someone becomes successful, families or friends might decide they are entitled to a piece of it. (Hint: they are not.) The entourage effect happens when these people, some of whom you barely know, come looking for a piece of the action.

I'll never forget: shortly after I signed a great contract with Cowboys, a family member who had never called me did. He let me know that his kid wanted a go-kart for Christmas that year. It took me about a half-second to figure out why this almost-total stranger was telling me this, but I decided to play it out:

"Why are you telling me this right now?"

He said, "Well, you know, if you're thinking about anything…"

"I've never bought you a Christmas present, ever. Why are you asking me for this for your kid right now?"

Then he does the "Well, I just… you know…" thing. He played it like we were all cool, best buddies and such. But I wasn't playing.

"I know exactly what you're doing and I'm not doing it," and the call pretty much ended there. Unfortunately, relatives and "friends" too often try to take advantage of you. People who are successful, who have produced something of value, take on a great responsibility—to use their success to support good causes. Many will try to guilt you into supporting their cause. Because you've made it and maybe, your brothers, sisters, or other family or friends haven't, it's often assumed that you need to take care of them.

Often, when trouble (real or perceived) arises, responsibility falls to whatever family or group member has the resources to deal with it. I've done that; I've helped people out. I've been super selective about it, but when that falls on you and you don't exercise any sort of emotional or physical control, others can try to take control in some way. You need to put clear boundaries and limits on what help you are willing to give.

It happens a lot with young athletes–plus singers, actors, inheritances, life insurance claims, and whoever else you can think of who joins the suddenly-rich crowd. They want to share, which is good, but they don't know how to do it right. I did this a couple of times: when family or friends went out, I bought dinner for everybody. Afterward, I thought, "That was dumb. Why couldn't they take care of their own bill? It's okay if I feel like I want to do something special once in a while, but do it too often and others will expect you to do it every time. They'll go from being grateful for your kindness to thinking they're entitled to your money. They're not and they need to understand that they're not my responsibility. My family (my wife and children) is my responsibility. Same goes for you. No one outside that small group has any claim on your personal assets. I'm sure you've felt the dinner scenario, too. Just know that it's on us individually to draw that boundary.

What about parents? Well, they've been adults longer than I have. They should have planned for themselves. If they haven't, or if circumstances are beyond their control–like a catastrophic health issue–come into play, then I'll certainly do what I can. The same goes for siblings and their families: not my responsibility. If I help them, it's not out of obligation, it's out of Christian charity.

That's a difference many people never learn, and many more hope you haven't learned. Beyond that:

1. If I have the resources to take care of others in need,
2. If I know that I have enough because I've done the planning and developed the discipline to do it right,

then I can, potentially, take care of some other people. It's an awesome feeling to step in and rescue those needing rescue. But we must take care of ourselves first.

You've probably heard the phrase, "Kill them with kindness." The entourage effect is that, in reverse, it's killing yourself with too much kindness toward others.

The Predator

I started this book talking about trust. It should be hard to earn. Well, sometimes, it isn't. The NFL, like many communities, I suppose, operates a lot on a referral basis. "Oh, I got this great financial advisor," says one player, "you should give her a call."

"I will," says another player, and it's done. No due diligence, just the word of a friend and trust is given. Bad plan.

A couple of running backs—"Jim" and "Larry"—signed up with this financial advisor who, somehow, got them to sign full powers of attorney so (she said) she could start moving money for them. She moved it alright, creating a whole set of separate, fake businesses and she moved cash among them. She created them to fund her lifestyle, not theirs, and so when they got out of the League, they found out that they didn't have any money. They came down on her, for sure, but there were unrecoverable losses due to money she'd spent.

"Sam," a big quarterback from Texas, moved back to Texas after playing in another state. He gave his uncle authority, a power of attorney, and discretion to spend. His uncle did just that, to the tune of $30 million. Sam worked years for that nest egg and when it was time to cook up an omelet, the nest was empty. It's your choice to be stupid with your money but at least, let it be your choice, not someone else's, to be stupid with your money. That's how these predators operate, making stupid sound brilliant.

When someone starts hinting, "Just trust me," I'm out, gone, bye, done, over you. I've had those conversations, and, over the years, I've had my wife to be the "second witness" (see 2 Corinthians 13:1). She and I have to be on the same page on all decisions or it's a hard no. I remember specifically, we were looking at this oil and gas deal we were planning to get involved in. I, by and large, was liking it—I was inclined to sign on. She was not. We've had lots of these discussions but on this one in particular, she simply said, "I don't like that guy."

"What about him? What do you mean?"

"He seems slimy to me." Good enough, and, just like that, I was out and I told him.

"What's the problem?" he asked.

"My wife doesn't like you. So, whatever it is about you, go fix it then come talk to us."

I'll be forever grateful I have a partner who's like that—intuitive and not at all shy about saying something's wrong when she felt off about a situation. Such a person is risk management embodied!

Here's the Thing

Most of the guys in the NFL are twenty-somethings; a few are thirty-somethings. I don't know how many guys were still playing in their forties, but let's call it (at most) a few dozen during the League's 100-plus years. They're drafted fresh out of college at age twenty-two or twenty-three. Today, I think the rookie league minimum is just short of $1 million. (Sometimes, I really want to be young and healthy again!) By comparison, the average US family income as I write this is around $75,000.

The money has changed a lot over the twenty years since I signed my first contract, but the rookies haven't changed much. Not many rich kids, that is; few pro athletes come from family wealth. We are in the game because we love it but also for that big paycheck. We're typically from lower- and middle-class families like mine. We're good at football (or basketball or baseball) and mostly, we're not good at engineering or medicine or whatever.

So, these guys come into the League and are very suddenly very wealthy. A million might be the minimum, but some of them get multi-million-dollar signing bonuses and a million or more for every game they play. That's money none of the "normal people" will ever see.

So, why doesn't the NFL step in and teach them how to manage their money?

They try.

The problem lies in the culture—lots of guys with lots of money and *very little life experience*. You see so many of those foolish behavior patterns in so many of these kids that the attitude ("I've got money, I'm having fun, it won't happen to me!") becomes like an addiction or a virus. The programs the NFL has just don't stick.

You have to be somebody that really cares. Brian Wansley (the Cowboys' director of player development) has brought me in for the last seven years in a row to tell my story. Other guys come in as well. The Cowboys' owner, Jerry Jones, sends his own chief financial officer (CFO) into these meetings to talk to new players. This is the guy who's in charge of all of their boss's billions, and they fall asleep!

Brian once told me, "I can only bring former players because only they are going to hit home with these guys." So, he brings former players in, but more than ninety percent of those stories are train-wreck stories, all about how you're going to get hurt in one way or another. I'm one of the guys who shares his story because mine isn't a train wreck.

The NFL treats you well—let's be clear about that. But there's a limit to what the League or anyone else can do. The rest is on you. You're over eighteen. You're an adult. It's time to act like one.

Most guys never learned about money growing up. But that's not an excuse; you can learn now. Pro sports is a microcosm. So while you've got that money making opportunity in your hands, use it to launch yourself into a higher trajectory.

Get around people who know more than you. Take their advice. Don't waste the chance while you've got it.

That's the advice I give to the Cowboy rookies every year. It's the same advice I give everybody because, as an old sage I know likes to say:

"Some things always work. Some things never work. Some people never learn the difference."

The Love of Money

Part of it is, I think, the natural, youthful invulnerability attitude, the feeling that "It can't happen to me"—until it does. These young bucks are all alpha males; they think they have a great deal of power because of their fame, their elite status in the sporting world, and because of the money they're getting. That power is an illusion. Unless you know what to do with it, power is always destructive; it poisons you. The Scriptures say:

> "For the love of money is the root of all evil: which while some coveted after, they have erred from the faith, and pierced themselves through with many sorrows."
>
> —1 Timothy 6:10

Not *money*, but *the love of money*. That's what everybody gets wrong and it holds true for power as well. People say things like, "He wasn't like this before he got rich." That's totally false—he was. Money didn't change him—whoever he becomes, he was already like that. That's a terrible thing to see, but it's just too often true. Money, like fame or skills or whatever, is nothing more than a resource. It allows some to do things that others can't because they don't have those resources.

Ever hear about the "televangelists"? They were preachers back in the 1980s who started broadcast ministries that turned into multimillion-dollar businesses. Names like Jim and Tammy Faye Bakker, Tony Alamo, Jimmy Swaggart were as well known as rock stars and pro athletes. They rose to fame like they were shot out of a bazooka and, when they fell, the craters were huge. Most of their careers ended after accusations over questionable fundraising or misuse of their power in regard to their female associates. Some of them ended up in jail. I mention them to illustrate a fact: if your pastor got weird after your church got bigger, your pastor was already weird.

It's all about who you are, not what you can do. Who you are comes from how your parents raised you, what you learned in church, or in other places where morality is—or is not—taught.

The good news is: you can change.

My Personal Transformation

The Realization

I didn't want to become another statistic, and it didn't take long for me to realize that Detroit was a place where that could easily happen. I've mentioned the gambling before—it was just one part of a broader locker room culture that didn't fit me.

As an undrafted guy, it was still a good opportunity to get on the field, so my agent and I agreed to a contract. Once I arrived, though, it became clear the environment wasn't the right one for me.

I had a lot of respect for Steve Mariucci. He was a genuine, player-first coach who looked out for his veterans—and that matters in a league where "veteran" can mean a guy who's lasted more than three seasons. I wanted to be that guy. But along with that, you also need a locker room that polices itself, and that part just wasn't there.

So I got lucky with an opportunity to move to Dallas and head coach Bill Parcells late that season. Parcells was "Sergeant City." He regularly patrolled the facility to see who was there. I would see him at 5:45 a.m. in the hot tub right before I was heading in to lift in the morning. Initially, only a few players went to the weight room daily; after a time, the whole team was there. That was Bill Parcells' definition of discipline.

He brought very different types of guys in, then set strict requirements for them. When guys proved they could handle it, he would give them more leash. Right there, Bill set a baseline performance, a foundational level to be able to win games. It was a mindset I respected and shared.

Where there was a lack of discipline, there was less success. The Lions went 5-11 in 2005, while the Cowboys went 9-7.

The Different Path

What does a pro football player do when the final gun goes off?

After my time with Miami and my move back to Texas, I had a conversation with the scouting staff. We were up in Jerry Jones's suite in the AT&T Stadium. It felt really impressive because the stadium was brand new, and this was the owner's private space, served by a private elevator that held maybe eight people. It was during the Cotton Bowl celebration, I think, and I was flirting with trying to join the scouting crew.

Tom Ciskowski, head scout at that time, asked if I was serious about scouting for the team. I said, "Yeah, I was thinking about it. I love to coach. I still love the team and the game."

"Do you love your family?"

"Yeah, obviously."

"Because you'll never see them."

Scouts go all over the country looking at college players, a part of the job that I hadn't fully considered. "Yeah, that makes sense." I knew that Tom already had this conversation with a buddy of mine, Marc Colombo. I remember sitting here thinking, "I love the game, love to coach, love being a part of it. I had sacrificed so much of my life for it already." I decided that I wanted more control over my work because I didn't want to be up till 2:00 a.m. or sleeping in my office at night, especially if I had a wife and children at home. Pro football offers so much great stuff, but it wasn't enough for me to sacrifice my family life to get it.

I also didn't want a coach lording over me. I could get on board with a Wade Phillips type of guy, who coached in the NFL for fifty years. He would shove guys out of the facility, saying, "Go home, be with your family!" But in most organizations, you essentially sacrifice months of your home life to be there, and I didn't want that. I wanted more control over when I came home.

That conversation in Jones's suite made that decision in my head. That was the start of me walking down this new professional path. It's great, because I'm actually enjoying football more, watching the games without any of the stress of being in the game.

Final Soundbites

Success without financial literacy is just delayed failure.

- **First**, build a river of wealth. Be excellent at your trade—athletes, craftsmen, professionals, you name it—and work to be the best at what you do.
- **Second**, build an income off your river of wealth—an income stream, or several, if you can. You start building up the streams along the way as you build the river, while proving to yourself that you can hold onto that money.
- **Third**, understand that "your money" is never all yours. Even if you blow it all away, like the rookie who got fined his whole salary, or those who gamble, or the one who bought a mega-mansion, others have claims. You will pay agents, business managers or accountants, and, of course, those wonderful boys and girls at the IRS who are watching *very* carefully.

Those who don't learn these rules become the statistics, the fifty percenters who make millions but have nothing left a half-decade after they retire. They proved they were good enough to earn it, and they proved they weren't smart enough to keep it.

CHAPTER 3

The Entrepreneurial Awakening

When Things Change, We Need to be Ready to Change with Them

Fundamental Ideas:

1. "Life is what happens while you're making other plans." (Old Joke)
2. "A house divided against itself cannot stand." (Abraham Lincoln)
3. All our problems have already happened to others and somebody has figured out a solution.

Finding Faith, Vision, and Voice

This is a long, somewhat complex, and deeply personal story, so bear with me.

I wasn't ready for my exit from the NFL. Mentally, I wasn't ready to be done, so life was challenging for me professionally for a while. I also mentioned my nephew's passing and the birth of our first child.

This created a huge spiritual turmoil inside me, among my family members, and at our church, where some members (I'll be restrained here) didn't live up to the Christian principles they professed. My brother and I left that church and haven't been back since. In fact, my attitude became typical of those who don't understand: "God? Yeah, I don't care about Him."

I understand this is a fight that a lot of people go through when they've lost somebody, especially a child. When somebody innocent gets taken out while all the trash is left in the world, you have to wonder, "Why?" This is a justifiable question, a good question to ask, and very common in the darkest times of life.

When the hospice nurse recommended that the family designate a representative from each side, so they didn't have to repeat the story or updates one hundred times to everybody, my side designated me, and my sister-in-law's family designated her sister. I went into full protector mode over my brother and his wife. I probably went way too aggressive on it, but he still thanks me today for warding off people.

The details aren't important; let's just say that all these stresses and others caused a lot of fractures within the family. Because of all this, I went into this very dark, don't-care-about-God mode.

Life went on. I took that sales job and after some time had passed, some friends invited us to a nondenominational church here in the Dallas-Fort Worth. We went in and, as I mentioned, I was more ready for a fight than a new connection to God.

I didn't get either, but during the worship, I did get punched in the face, spiritually speaking. I "saw" my nephew, Evan, who'd passed away, like he was sitting on God's lap. I didn't get any audible communication, but I had this overwhelming peaceful feeling, as if God said to me, "I've got him, he's good."

It was just to me—a private thing—and it caused me to think, "I want a piece of that." Just enough of the wall came down that day where I could come back the next week and hear the Word, as Paul wrote:

> So then faith cometh by hearing, and hearing by the word of God.
>
> —Romans 10:17

Over the weeks that followed, I did return and piece by piece, I started listening to the message and ultimately, gave my life to Christ, being baptized into that church. (I had been baptized into my former church years before, but that was as a child. This time, I made my choice as a man to walk this path.)

During that time, I was pounded with revelation. I became an insane consumer of Scripture messages, TED Talks, your story, their stories—anything I could get my hands on to help build my faith. That's when I became the devoted (some say "insane") reader. I was beginning to truly understand what all those people were talking about when they quoted:

> Trust in the LORD with all thine heart; and lean not unto thine own understanding.
>
> —Proverbs 3:5

I don't want this book to become a sermon, but I do want to emphasize a couple of things in this spiritual journey that directly relate to my later professional journey. First, as I became more tuned-in spiritually, something of significance hit me square in the face: I now believed in God—that there was one, and I wasn't Him. Second, I was trying to carry the full weight of closing the door on football, my nephew's brief life, my daughter's new life, and leaving my former church association. I was also trying to carry the full weight of my family all on my own. Carrying all that became too much for me to bear.

I was happy to do so because that's what men—fathers, brothers, protector-providers—do, right?

Wrong. A lot of guys do, that is, they try, and it's too much, and it breaks them. As I walked along this new spiritual path, I felt, for the first time, like God was telling me, "Don't try to bear all this; put it on Me. You and I will carry it together."

That became an essential element at a critical time for me. Understanding this idea allowed me—the big, tough jock—to give my life to Christ and let Him share the burden. That understanding also led me to professional lessons:

1. Jesus qualified Himself to be Christ (which you can read about in Hebrews 5) by the things He suffered and became able to ease our burdens if we share them with Him. I later qualified myself to ease people's financial burdens through education and experience. If others will let me share my financial expertise with them, I can guide them to the right financial decisions just as the Scriptures guide us toward a righteous life. I'm not comparing myself to Christ in any way, except to say that His example—how and what He did—has applications to our lives outside religion.
2. In giving my life to Christ, I gave Him the opportunity to pound me with those revelations that allowed me

to take out a lot of the trash that I'd brought with me from previous experiences. I could then reconcile with, and ultimately gain access to, the vision that He had for my life. That vision of helping others led me to where I am.

My walk back to faith reconciled me to Evan's death with the fact that he was not "lost" but "elsewhere," and he was okay. I also began developing useful attributes and though I wasn't yet a leader, I was getting ready to lead.

As my experiences and awakening became known, I started receiving invitations to speak, to share my testimony, my faith, and everything that was happening to me. As those invitations came, a clear impression also came to mind, "Remember the wreck." (In particular, the part about me being a selfish teenager thinking mostly about how that day affected my life and how it took more than a year to realize how much it had affected others.) So I started diving into it, and that became a key moment in my spiritual rebirth. It was like God said to me, "Okay, here's what it is: this is what you've done in life. Now go repeat it, but without the ego."

That struck me hard but, after much reflection on my pre-faith life, I realized that, even though I was a good worker, I was still very self-centered. All my anger with God over Evan was my way of saying, "God, why did You do this terrible thing *to me*?" I was making assumptions about God's plan for us and assuming that Evan's death was a bad thing. But he's now in God's hands, safe from the world. I should have been celebrating the fact that we had him with us for that short time, not blaming God for sparing him most of life's troubles.

That shift in perspective–from "what happened to me" to "what can I do with this"–became the foundation of everything that followed.

Losing Evan didn't just change my relationship with God. It fundamentally altered how I approached every area of my life, especially business. I started asking different questions. Instead of "How do I get more?" I asked, "How can I protect what matters?" Instead of "How do I succeed?" I asked, "How can I build something that outlasts me?"

The NFL had taught me that success without protection is temporary. Now my faith was teaching me that pain without purpose is wasted. I realized that Evan's brief life–and my family's response to losing him–held lessons I could use to help others avoid the financial train wrecks I'd witnessed in locker rooms and boardrooms alike.

Every client who walked through my door after that was dealing with their own version of what my family faced: unexpected crises, uncontrollable circumstances, and the desperate need for someone who understood that money isn't just about accumulation–it's about protection, continuity, and legacy.

I couldn't control what happened to Evan. But I could control how I responded. And I could use what I learned to make sure other families never had to face financial devastation on top of personal tragedy.

That became my mission. That's what drove me to build Pro Capital around a single question: "What if the worst happens–will your family be okay?"

Translating a Spiritual Journey into Speaking with Substance and Energy

> A man's gift maketh room for him, and bringeth him before great men.
>
> —Proverbs 18:16

As I read the Scriptures, I realized that God had brought people into my life for a purpose. Well, if we're sitting in a group, the turn eventually comes around to me to speak. If I haven't crafted my gift, if I haven't developed it and put my thoughts together in order then I'm going to say something stupid. I'm going to be seen as a fool at the gate, and others will think, "You idiot, you had nothing to contribute to this conversation."

In my previous profession, I developed some wisdom regarding my craft. I learned plays and how to read an offense, and, now, how to manage money. I needed to be better at telling people about all this.

Now, I don't have any private revelation on this, but let's imagine a possibility: what if Evan had a conversation with God before he came into our family? God said, "Your family's going to stray from the path. It'll take something big to get their attention. Are you willing to be that something, even if it's really hard?" Evan says, "If it's for my family, I can do it," and he comes to us for a short time. When his mission is done, God calls him home.

Even if we were sure something like that happened, it doesn't fix the pain we feel at losing him. It does provide a totally different spin on what I do about it. I'm going to say, "Okay, well, if that's the case, and he made a choice, I'm going to make sure his sacrifice wasn't for nothing." That realization gave me the momentum I needed to move on. That's also why, in casual conversations over coffee or something, I share my story and testimony and someone says, "You need to share this with my little group," I can.

Then I go to that small group and, when I'm done, one or two of them says, "You need to talk to my people." Suddenly, from a one-on-one conversation, I'm traveling to Israel, speaking at the Robert K. Kraft Field at Lawrence A. Wien Stadium (through a Hebrew translator) in Israel!

From there, it's Barcelona to talk to a faith-based football camp. Then, I'm climbing Mount Kilimanjaro in Africa, sharing my testimony with a group on the side of the mountain. Not long after that, I'm addressing a men's conference of 8,000 guys in Springfield, Missouri.

I'm thinking, "What the heck's happening right now?" I'm sharing a great message but there are also financial considerations because airfare and hotels and meals have to be considered. Things keep moving fast, and, I confess, I got a little overbearing about my faith, to the point where I could hear the Spirit telling me to step on the brakes.

So, in the middle of all this, I got recommended as a financial advisor to a gentleman, who was a retired widower. His daughter introduced him to me, and he came aboard as a client. I put a plan together, got all his stuff in order. He was impressed by our proposal and after meeting with a couple of other advisors, he chose my firm, and it's been really good for both of us.

We implemented the plan and afterwards, we had a sit-down review. We're sipping coffee in the office, and he shared that he'd started dating a woman. Well, his kids didn't like this, because he was married to their mother for fifty years before she passed. I'm not sure where our conversation was going, but I followed him  and he was really opening up.

We had a faith-based conversation in which the Spirit was so thick I couldn't do anything but listen. He started sharing elements of his faith, including the fact that his daughter had lost her husband just a few weeks earlier—a man in his mid-forties with ten and twelve-year-old children. In helping his daughter out, he brought some paperwork for us to look at and said, "Take care of my daughter."

That hit me like an NFL defensive line. (If something like that man's story and plea doesn't hit you, then I don't know what will.) This was one of those times where you see financials collide with life. The money was an extension of his family—a representation of a life. When life is lost or comes close to the edge, you finally start to understand how fragile it is. Money works the same. Most people think they could handle $400 million but have zero sense of its fragile nature. If it's not handled well, it has a way of just disappearing into the night. Like a life that's close to the edge, we don't think about it until we brush up against it or lose it. That's when you realize it's not the sins of *commission* but the sins of *omission* that haunt us. That's when we wake up from our slumber and start to take it seriously.

This is what I'd seen all these times when revelation hit me and how it turned practical advice into guidance for working with money. I began to see that all these experiences were blending together–spiritually, practically, and professionally.

People were getting to know me through my testimony and respecting me because I knew my profession. Through that profession, I had opportunities to truly affect, in a positive way, their practicality, giving them opportunities to progress in other areas, including spiritual things.

More of the Same

Like football and finance, it didn't just happen. It took work.

I started getting asked to speak about my faith because people recognized and respected the fire of my faith. Then, as people got to know more about me, they asked me to speak about football and money. That's a very different skill set from testifying. I needed to develop that craft, to present myself realistically but professionally. I had to learn which stories hit and which missed, which made people laugh and which didn't. I fell flat more than a few times and needed to learn how to recover from a bad joke.

By creating and executing a plan, then doing it, failing at it, and doing it again and again until I got it right, I found out what worked for me. That unleashed my vision, to do good for other people in any way I could. All of a sudden, it became something explosive. The whole program expanded very quickly. In response, I thought, "Well, I need to meet explosive people." So, I talked with different people who had built explosively successful companies and started applying their success methods to my business.

The Family Complexity

Divorces, Multiple Marriages, and Blended Families

While all of that was going on, I had ongoing family issues.

As I've mentioned in a previous chapter, Clay, Casey, and I are the sons of our parents' second marriages. Their first marriages produced no children, but their third marriages brought step-siblings into the family. My stepmom had several children. I never lived with any of them and only had enough contact with two of her daughters to have any sort of a relationship with them. I mentioned Charlie's kids and six growing children sharing one bathroom. There were other challenges.

Charlie passed away about two years ago. Having been married nearly thirty years, there was the natural comingling of assets, and, so all of a sudden, Mom was the evil stepmom to the stepchildren. For example, who stepped up to pay the funeral bill? It wasn't very expensive, but it was just over $13,000. I wasn't going to let my mom foot that bill alone. I've never known her financial situation—she's still very private about all that—but I wasn't going to let her go into debt right after losing her husband.

I'm not going to judge, but my stepsiblings were very upset that she cancelled his cell service almost immediately. (Why should she keep paying for it?) They said they wanted to listen to his voicemails. So, I sent the bill for the funeral over text to all the siblings, since Mom became the target of some choice words.

I thought I was being reasonable: you have to buy into the table to be part of the discussions and decisions. Do you think any of our step-siblings (his own children) stepped up to contribute to the bill? If you guessed "no," you'd be correct. My brothers and I paid for our stepfather's funeral, and that was that.

Life happens. It can be complex, and my family had complexities on both sides. All of this has to be managed, even in the worst of times. Where money is concerned, everybody wants it, no one wants to contribute it, and in the final analysis, the responsibility usually falls on whoever has the most of it.

Speaking generally, you've probably noticed that there are plenty of greedy rich people, as well as greedy not-rich people. Those people mostly don't want to help others. The people we want to work for or with are those who take on an extra load on top of their own burdens and do it intentionally—those who think, "God's blessed me with this, so I have to do good with it. I don't want to give to somebody who's just greedy, but it's never about them; it's always about me, doing what's right."

At times, the person with the money has to step up and make sure that other people are taken care of—a funeral, medical bills, a temporary home—filling whatever need arises. Most of us don't have that proverbial "rich uncle" who can step in. Most of us aren't that rich uncle. In those cases, their church community can help, collecting small donations to solve big problems. First, though, it should be the family. We need to take care of our own.

We have times when family members say, "There's no way I'm giving money to my brother. He's an idiot." That's reasonable—if they won't use your generosity to help solve their problems, you're not helping, you're enabling. Like the homeless person on the street. Don't give them money—they might use on booze or drugs. Buy them a meal or rent them a room instead; that's just simple logic, and there are a lot of times when people should step up. When others haven't made it like we have, financially speaking, if I can help see that everything's taken care of, then I'm happy to do so.

That's very much the way I feel about my brother, Casey. I offered to help after he and his wife lost Evan. The oncologist at St. Jude told them to take him home and predicted he had two months left. (He actually made it about thirty days.) The doctor also (maybe with a little help from God) encouraged them to have more children. He warned them that Evan's cancer had a genetic component, but he'd been through many similar cases, and he gave them high odds, like one in two million, against a repeat of the cancer. Well, Casey and his wife were scared to death to try for more, fearing the worst.

Her doctor suggested altering her birth control, which meant a month without any to get her body ready for the new treatment. Well, you can guess how that turned out with a young, healthy couple. Like a cliché movie script, she got pregnant with twins! Now, they have two very healthy little tornadoes running around their house. I told them I'd pay for private school for the girls if they'd move to Texas so I could be closer to my wonderful little nieces (and to get my family away from the crazy politics in Washington state).

The Point: Have You Planned for It?

I repeat the old joke: "Life is what happens while you're busy making other plans."

These days, unfortunately, most people seem to think, "Life happens, and you don't have to plan for it." They generally end up as the punch line of a very bad joke.

Life is complex; it mixes a 1950s musical where everybody lives happily ever after with that 1970s slasher movie where something evil always lurks behind every door, plus all the situations in between. Whatever you're experiencing at any given moment, all of it comes with a price tag. In addition to the happy days you create, tough times happen that most of us never anticipate:

- **America's now facing its largest senior population ever.** By 2029, when the youngest Baby Boomers turn sixty-five, more than twenty percent of the US population will be age sixty-five or older (Georgetown Center on Retirement Research, 2018). The oldest Boomers are already nearing eighty. Someone turning sixty-five today has nearly a seventy percent chance of needing some type of long-term care services (Administration for Community Living, ACL.gov). That could mean hosting a parent in your home, hiring part-time help for them, or paying for a private room in a facility. The median national cost for a private nursing home room now exceeds $116,000 per year, with high-end markets running significantly more (MarketWatch, 2024).
- Many grandparents now provide temporary care for grandchildren or are raising them completely. Younger couples might have to take on a niece, nephew, or godchild unexpectedly. That could mean renovating your house or buying a larger home. It'll mean changes to the monthly budget, funding more college educations, and perhaps even caring for a child with a disability.

- Divorce frequently ends with one of the spouses in bankruptcy. Remarriages can bring stepchildren–and bitter ex-spouses–into the picture. Who bears the financial responsibilities, for whom, and for what? When do those bills come due?
- Despite your best efforts, some investments go bad. Your employer might go belly up, get bought out, or need to reduce staff. You, your spouse, or your children might face a lawsuit, an accident, an illness, or any of the hundreds of bad-news scenarios we see every day in the news.
- Family members can face all the problems you can face, and you may feel a moral obligation to help–unless that relative is an addict, an "entourage" hanger-on, or something. (Christian charity and enabling bad behavior don't mix.) But medical emergencies, loss of jobs, funeral costs, and similar situations are circumstances where we legitimately need to step in and assist however we can.

Gen X and Millennials are now what some are calling "the sandwich generations." We're in the middle years, still raising our children while dealing with aging parents.

There are many ways to deal with these possibilities. We have insurance, investments, and other vehicles that help us "put something away for a rainy day." We have LLCs, trusts, and many other options for protecting our assets when disasters strike. I repeat: it isn't about how much you can earn; it's about how much you can keep. That's the key to reality-based financial planning.

As I've secured greater success, I've felt a motivation to help my siblings and others. Maybe, as I've gotten closer to God, He's opened up my heart to the truth of the Second Great

Commandment, "Thou shalt love thy neighbour as thyself."
(Matthew 22:39).

The recent hurricane damage in western North Carolina
and floods in Texas really have brought out the best on
some of us. I see so many instances of people jumping in
wherever they can and giving generously that I have to think
it's natural to most of us. I may never figure it all out, and I
guess it doesn't really matter. I can work like it's all up to me
and pray like it's all up to Him, so I do.

In more normal circumstances, I actively recruit team
members who can help me help others create and execute
solid financial plans. If we, the planning industry, do what
we should be doing, we can help the sandwich generation
deal with life's surprises without ruining the finances of all
the generations.

I'm constantly thinking, "God, bring me the people You want
on this path." By "people," I mean those who need my help
and those who can help me. In very practical terms, this is
where our firm and our expertise step in and manages all
these boogeymen.

Summary

My spiritual experience gave me something of a missionary
zeal to get my message out. Initially, that was a spiritual message, which people responded to enthusiastically. That led
to business discussions with people who liked what I had to
say and responded with, "I want to hear more about this."

I developed the business message as I looked back on my
family's financial problems and the problems I saw among
players in the NFL. I saw that these problems weren't unique

and that my experience was not unique. Almost everybody deals with those same problems. That meant there were solutions that could apply to many people. I'm now growing my business with checklists of things to do in specific situations. I know which things work and which things don't because I've been through them and helped many others through them.

CHAPTER 4

THE WEALTH DESTRUCTION EPIDEMIC

Why Ninety Percent of Wealthy Families Lose Everything by the Third Generation

Fundamental Ideas:

1. Lawsuits are the most destructive attacks on personal and family wealth.
2. The government does what is best for the government, not for you.
3. *Conventional wisdom* (what everybody "knows" is true) often isn't wisdom or truth.

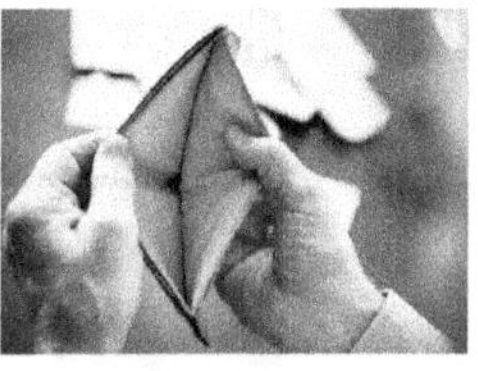

Public Domain Illustration

Shocking Statistics

- The older generations are expected to transfer $84 trillion in wealth by 2045.[4]

---

[4] Pam Krueger. "The $84 Trillion Question–Will Your Family's Wealth Last or Disappear?" *Worth.com*. New York City: Worth Media Group, 16 June 2025. https://worth.com/84-trillion-wealth-transfer-will-your-familys-wealth-last-or-disappear

- Seventy percent of wealthy families lose their wealth by the second generation; ninety percent lose it by the third.[5]
- Most successful entrepreneurs die broke or leave their families vulnerable.[6]

Why? As previously mentioned, many financial advisors focus on the money they manage instead of on the risks to that wealth.

Lawsuit Disasters

According to various studies:

- **More than forty million lawsuits are filed every year in the United States** (One Legal, 2023). Some legal analysts suggest that when you include all state court filings, the number may exceed **one hundred million annually** (Blake Harris Law, 2023).

- **Seventy-five percent of middle-class Americans are never sued**, while the remaining twenty-five percent face at least one lawsuit in a given year (Law Stack Exchange, 2022).

---

[5] Unbylined, "Generational Wealth: Why do 70% of Families Lose Their Wealth in the 2nd Generation?" *Nasdaq.com*. New York City: Nasdaq. 19 October 2018. https://www.nasdaq.com/articles/generational-wealth%3A-why-do-70-of-families-lose-their-wealth-in-the-2nd-generation-2018-10

[6] Lorie Konish, "67% of Americans have no estate plan, survey finds," *CNBC.com*. Englewood Cliffs, NJ: CNBC, 11 April 2022. https://www.cnbc.com/2022/04/11/67percent-of-americans-have-no-estate-plan-heres-how-to-get-started-on-one.html

- Based on these estimates, Americans are far more likely than citizens in most nations to be involved in a lawsuit at some point in their lives.

Truthfully, there's no reason to feel comfortable with any of those conclusions, unless you've prepared your family and assets to withstand as much of the damage a lawsuit can as possible.

One thing is certain—those with more wealth have a greater shot at a day in court. They have more assets (homes, businesses, etc.) and alleged "victims" are more likely to sue because they think they're more likely to get something out of a rich person than a poor person.

In other areas, the stats are firmer: expect three or four auto accidents during your driving lifetime. That's why every driver is required by law to have auto insurance (Anthem Injury Lawyers, 2024). About one-quarter to one-third of all law enforcement officers (LEOs) fire their weapons in the line of duty during their careers, but every LEO carries on duty, and most carry off duty (Guns.com, 2017). Remember the old adages:

Better to have it and not need it than to need it and not have it.

Your odds might be one in a million but if you're the one, you don't care about anybody else.

What you spend on creating and maintaining a solid estate plan is nothing more than insurance. Entrepreneurs organize businesses to create what's called "the veil of protection" to separate personal assets from business assets so that whatever happens to the business doesn't affect those personal assets.

Metaphorically, the family business is like a newborn baby. You do everything for it, and you hover over it lovingly because it has captured your heart. In practical terms, it's often the most important asset on the family books. Many business owners are depending on that business for their livelihood, retirement, inheritance, and everything else. Even if they have other resources—such as land, IRAs, a stock portfolio—the business, they hope, will eventually be more valuable than those others. And maybe you're like me, but I'm not interested in someone thinking they have a lawsuit pay day if I make a mistake.

Michelle, Marleigh, and Me

I tell people that most of us are "one accident away from zero," and much of that depends on our wealth. Few of us are going to waste time with a million-dollar lawsuit against a minimum-wage earner. If you can afford to live in an affluent neighborhood, however, you have a larger target on your back. It comes with the territory. For example, we live in an area where the average household income is over $200,000 per year. That typically comes with higher valued homes and newer cars. Our kids go to a private school, with a daily car show in the parking lot—and I don't mean the parents' drop-off lane. Around our area, most of the kids drive nicer vehicles simply because our neighborhood has the discretionary income to afford it.

The point being, the larger the perceived or actual net worth equals the larger target, and not just for outsiders. Did you hear about Dr. "Michelle," the plastic surgeon who got into an accident? The other driver was found to be at fault, and the doctor sued for $30 million! Her hands were injured, ending her surgical career (it could've been the inspiration for *Doctor Strange*), and the court decided that her lost wages, pain and suffering, and so on qualified for the payout.

So, if you were in that same scenario and hit the plastic surgeon who lost out on a great income stream, where are they taking the money from? Your brokerage account? Your bank account? Investment properties? Most people say insurance, but if you have $1 million in liability coverage, you still have the majority payout remaining. You have to cover that.

A common scenario is this: a husband and wife came to us. They owned five rental properties, all with their names on the titles. They had about $8 million in their brokerage account. They owned a business. If those assets aren't properly restructured, all of them would be part of the personal wealth that might have become property owned by "Michelle" had they been the defendants in that lawsuit.

By the way, it doesn't have to be that dramatic. What's the plan if a renter falls and breaks a leg, then decides to go after the property owners? How much liability insurance did they have on each property? Are the properties all held under a single LLC? Each property should be in a separate LLC so that one disaster doesn't spill over into all your other holdings.

Now, it could be even worse than just losing assets. "Marleigh" was nineteen when she went to a party and had one beer. Legally, she wasn't intoxicated but she was drinking underage (it's twenty-one in most places). When she hit another car, resulting in a fatal injury, the fallout was like an atomic bomb! Her family's insurance policy was voided because of the underage drinking, putting her family on the losing side of a massive lawsuit. Fortunately, a carefully crafted asset-protection plan saved the family's finances, but the girl still did jail time. (Imagine getting a felony conviction at age nineteen, knowing you'll carry it for the rest of your life.)

But let's get even more ordinary in our circumstances. I was out walking our dog with our daughter not long ago. Another resident was also walking their dog. On the football field, you always keep your eyes open for the guy who's going to try and pound you into the ground like a tent stake. We called it "keeping your head on a swivel." On that day, I noticed the neighbor had a tight hold on a very stout leash and harness. I repeat some sage advice: "A measured paranoia is a vital survival skill."

That other dog got aggressive suddenly but having seen the signs, I was able to get my daughter and our dog out of the other dog's reach before there was a problem. That other dog was prone to fighting, and the owner knew it. Even so, if her dog attacked mine and my dog won the fight, she could sue me for those injuries, plus mental anguish and anything else. If I could prove she knew the dog was aggressive–with neighbors who'd witnessed past attacks–she probably wouldn't win. However, court is where the truth is decided, in most cases. Anybody can file a suit, and many people file frivolous lawsuits, guessing that you'd rather spend $50,000 to settle than to risk losing $1 million in a trial. (Often, they're right.)

Regardless of how a lawsuit ends, you've lost time, effort, and money defending yourself. Lawsuits frequently bring justice to those harmed, but not always. And even if you're completely in the right, the jury can rule against you. "Your day in court" is no different than a day at a casino. You can win big, or you can lose it all.

Taxes and Succession in a Business

"Irene" is one of our Texas real estate moguls, a very successful woman. She's an older gal on her fourth marriage (they file separately), and she's estranged from her children. Irene came to us with a $32 million net worth: $20 million in the business, $11 million in real estate, and $1 million in an IRA.

Suppose she were to die today intestate. First, let's dispel a myth—*no one dies intestate*! Whatever state you live in has, by statute, rules that govern distribution of your estate if you have not written a will. In effect, the state has written a will for you. If you don't clearly express your wishes for the distribution of your assets when you die, a judge will do it for you, and he or she doesn't care what you wanted—only what state statute says.

So, Irene passes on, and the state—specifically the probate court—takes control. The federal government and the state collect the taxes due them. Then all the outstanding bills are paid. Finally, whatever is left is handed out to the heirs—the spouse and children.

Bad plan—and it's so obviously a bad plan that two-thirds of Americans haven't done anything about it.

(Sarcasm there, in case you missed it.)

First, the taxes: the federal estate tax (commonly called an "inheritance tax" or "death tax") is forty percent of all assets over a specified amount—$13.6 million in 2025. That means $17.4 million of Irene's estate is taxable, to the tune of just under $7 million. Texas and thirty-seven other states have no estate tax, so she is safe on that score. Vermont, on the other hand, exempts $5 million in assets from their tax, imposing a flat tax of sixteen percent to everything over that amount. For Irene, that's sixteen percent of $27 million, about $4.32 million.

Between her state and federal taxes, Irene might lose more than $11 million—a full third of her estate—to the government. Talk about penalizing success!

In addition, none of her children have any experience or interest in real estate, but she has a team of dedicated, skilled employees who've helped her build this little empire. What do they get when she passes? Pink slips. The only avenue to paying those taxes is liquidation of the business and her real estate holdings and the employees get nothing.

Fire sale time! Probate records are public court records; everybody who cares to look has access to them. Everyone will know that her heirs need cash for taxes and they need to sell fast. Not even your best friend would offer fair market value under those circumstances. Irene is in her seventies, and life has been pretty good to her, but suppose we added an abusive marriage, vindictive ex-spouses, several step-children, or any one of a dozen other possible complications. This worst-case scenario gets even worse very fast. So let's keep it simple.

We're presented with two challenges. First, secure the estate to avoid as much taxation as possible. Second, secure the business so that the employees and clients are protected.

Regarding the estate, there's a wide variety of options. If everything is titled as personal property of Irene, then it's all part of her estate. Placing assets in trusts means the trust sends your assets where you've directed them. Did the marriages include stepchildren? Does Irene want to include them or exclude some of her children from inheriting? A friend of mine has never married or had children. He has a relationship with a goddaughter that's stronger than any with his nieces or nephews. He also has grand-nieces and grandnephews with disabilities. A "pretermitted children" clause in a will specifies which children will inherit and which are *disowned*, as they used to say. He could designate as his heirs this goddaughter or those grandnieces and grandnephews with disabilities. If a "love child" appeared, that child could be specifically omitted, included, or limited.

Second, securing the business. Her employees helped her create her wealth; she cares about them and wants them to continue servicing her clients, who were also key to her wealth. As noted, if the children have to sell off company assets to pay taxes, they'll get little or nothing for their years of service. She needs a business organization that will survive her. She could form a corporation, give stock to key performers, create a board of directors, and set rules for succession that are clear and firm and separate from her assets as an individual.

A short aside: years ago, an insurance company and a bank got together. Both were publicly traded companies and giants in their local market, but their leaders wanted to be sure those businesses stayed focused locally, instead of becoming part of giant conglomerates. So they made a stock trade: the bank acquired fifty-one percent of the insurance stock and the insurance acquired fifty-one percent of the bank stock. The merger agreement included a clause requiring that less than half the board members of each company be board members of the other company, providing a serious watchdog scenario, with other provision that guaranteed that neither company could be bought out by a national firm. They remain, to this day, locally-oriented businesses.

You probably don't have to be that creative to secure the future of your business, but you do need to take advantage of every protection available.

One final thought—and most people think of this as a nightmare—but it isn't; it's necessary honesty. You need to be open with family and others about your plans. Most people don't want to think about losing Mom or Dad, but you need to be realistic: it is going to happen. Discuss your final plans with your spouse and children. If they don't know what you want, they'll do what they want, just like the state. Designate an executor, inform them where to find the documents, the keys, and all PINs and passwords! Also, if children don't have a good relationship with their parents, it's highly probable that they don't have a good relationship with each other. All sorts of idiotic excuses can be imagined for why the firstborn or fourth daughter should get more than the others—or why one should get it all.

You might've heard of a novel by Charles Dickens entitled *Bleak House*. Set in the early 1800s, the story revolves around a family probate case, *Jarndyce vs. Jarndyce*. The original Jarndyce wrote conflicting wills and the heirs fought for decades over which one was legitimate. The book ends with the case being resolved but sadly, lawyer fees and court costs left the estate empty. That entire fight was for nothing! Dickens, by the way, based his novel, in part, on a real lawsuit from 1797 which was contested and not settled until 1859! Legal professionals criticized Dickens's satire as exaggerated but the novel became a rallying point for judicial reforms enacted by Parliament in the 1870s.

If it isn't done right, chances are that no one will profit except the lawyers.

Switching Gears

I have a client—a couple with a healthy estate—who came to me saying they had "reached a cap" with their current advisor. I've heard that comment before; it's all too common in the financial industry. They hadn't done any asset protection in their planning. My firm coordinated with their accountant who told me, "Oh, no, no need to worry about that. They've already got those documents." I went back to the couple. They were sure they'd never created any such documents.

After a couple of rounds of this and some serious research on everybody's part, guess what? The CPA was wrong. He wasn't being dishonest or trying to scam anybody; he just made a normal human mistake. We all do it. Nobody got unduly upset because he was, other than this little mishap, a good accountant. We simply had to correct the mistake.

Another common mistake after creating a set of documents is the assumption they'll last forever. Every three to five years, or when a major life change occurs, you need to review and update all documents, making sure they reflect your current situation. Especially when a marriage or divorce occurs, when children are born, when you stop being a paycheck employee and become an entrepreneur, or when you retire, the rules change.

And while I'm at it, Congress or your state legislature can change the rules any time they're in session. It doesn't hurt to get acquainted with your legislators and keep yourself informed about what changes are being discussed in "the halls of power." If you feel that strongly about it, consider running for office yourself. You might pay little or no attention to politics, but I guarantee they take an interest in you—and your money!

Rethinking "Impossible" as a Concept

You might think these worst-case scenarios are impossible, that no successful businessperson would neglect planning so thoroughly. You'd be wrong. We're now living in the early years of the greatest wealth transfer in history, as baby boomers and their parents begin passing their wealth to Generations X, Y, and Z. As mentioned earlier, one report estimates that $84 trillion in assets will change hands over the next twenty years, with about $12 trillion going to charity and $72 trillion to heirs.[7] Trustandwill.com estimates that less than one-third of Americans even have a will, that just eleven percent have a trust, and fifty-five percent have no estate plan at all.[8]

---

[7] Joseph Coughlin, "The Great Wealth Transfer is Happening but not in the Way You Think," *Forbes.com*. Jersey City, New Jersey: Integrated Whale Media Investments, 26 June 2024 (updated 17 December 2024). https://www.forbes.com/sites/josephcoughlin/2024/06/26/the-great-wealth-transfer-is-happening-but-not-in-the-way-you-think/, accessed 11 August 2025.

[8] Staff, "Who Has an Estate Plan? A Demographic Breakdown," *TrustAndWill.com*. San Diego: Trust&Will, (undated). https://trustandwill.com/learn/2025-report-estate-planning-demographic-breakdown/, accessed 11 August 2025.

This is definitely not an area where following the crowd will get you somewhere you want to be.

Family and Friends Destruction

As I said, probate creates two problems. First, it's a very public process, so everybody knows your business. Second, the court controls the outcome, not you, so anyone can claim anything. The court has no way to know, beforehand, what's true and what's not. Every potential heir or claimant gets their due process.

I also remind you of the "entourage" effect. The hands come out when there are assets to be claimed. This happened to my uncle Hap when he passed away. It felt like everybody who knew him came around, saying things like, "Hey, Hap told me he would give me this piece of land." "He said he'd give me a couple acres because I helped him out one time." "You know, he told me he'd give me 500 bucks or 5,000 bucks for helping him out with this or that problem." Whatever they want to claim, there's no paper and no family-friendly witnesses, so they can claim anything. If they're lying, it's certain they can find "witnesses" to back their false claim. Defending against those claims can be very expensive.

I saw this in my life and many other players in the NFL, so I'm especially sensitive to it, but everybody should recognize the possibility. Most people—the vast, overwhelming majority—are honest, and this sort of scam would never cross their minds. Still, it only needs to cross one mind to ruin your day. If you have somebody savvy enough (and crooked enough) to go to the court and file a contest, you should know they have a fighting chance.

As you increase in assets, trouble is around every corner. Planning ensures safety for everybody concerned.

The Wall Street Lie

The Myth

Over the last 150 years, the US stock market has averaged a positive annual return far ahead of most others, making the stock market one of the best places to put your money.

The Reality

First, you haven't been in the stock market for 150 years.

Second, not every stock does that well.

The Index Fund Trap

One thing people don't think about is assets that don't produce income.

These are assets that *might* appreciate over time but don't kick off any cash flow today. Think about companies like Amazon, NVIDIA, or Tesla early on. They took years, sometimes decades, before they were consistently profitable. Along the way, they didn't pay dividends. They just sat there while investors waited on the "someday."

That's the bet. You're buying growth on speculation. You're saying, "I believe this company will be worth a lot more in the future," even though there's no income coming back to you right now. You're not buying it for cash flow—you're buying it because you hope that a $10 share turns into a $1,000 share five or ten years down the road.

But here's the problem: if you need money before that big day arrives, your only option is to *sell the asset* or *borrow against it.* Either way, you're giving something up. That big score you were waiting on? You just took a chunk out of it. You can't pull income directly out of a stock any more than you can pull one wall out of your house and use it to pay the bills.

Now, sure, those who saw the future clearly and picked the right companies were rewarded handsomely. But the hard truth is this: you don't know *when* that someday will come… or if it ever will.

Index funds absolutely have a place in a portfolio. They can be a great tool. But like everything else in life, they can be overused. And when too much of your wealth is tied up in assets that don't pay you, you're not building freedom, you're just waiting on hope.

The Do-It-Yourself Trap

I'm pretty agnostic when it comes to investments. I don't care what the *thing* is. I care whether it solves the problem or moves me closer to the goal. That's it.

Some people are true DIY investors. They like reading stock reports, tracking indexes, following news cycles, and checking account values. They know exactly how much is in their brokerage account, what each investment is "supposed" to do, what their house is worth, and how all of it fits into their picture of retirement. Those are good things—to a point.

The issue isn't awareness. The issue is *management.*

One of the biggest trends on Wall Street is that retirement planning is as simple as picking a 70/30, 60/40, or 50/50 split between stocks and bonds and calling it a day. Stocks and bonds are just two tools, and there are a lot more than two.

Real diversification means spreading risk across *different kinds* of assets, not just different tickers. That can include insurance, rental real estate (residential or commercial), businesses, or even assets like precious metals, which don't produce income but do tend to hold purchasing power over time. There are also equity-based strategies beyond traditional public markets. The list is long.

The old saying about not putting all your eggs in one basket applies just as much on Wall Street as it does on a farm.

Here's the part most people don't like to admit: many Americans have wealth but no real plan behind it. And that's understandable. If you're a doctor, an engineer, a business owner, a writer—whatever your craft is—your time is valuable. If you're earning hundreds or thousands of dollars an hour doing what you're good at, spending that time trying to master every corner of investing probably isn't the best use of it.

I've hired a writing coach. I've hired a lawyer. I've hired people to do things I *could* try to learn—but shouldn't. They do it better, faster, and usually cheaper in the long run than I ever could. Money works the same way. That doesn't mean you should be disconnected or uninformed. It just means you don't have to do everything yourself.

At Pro Capital, we've built what we call the **VAULT™ Method**, a five-pillar framework designed to organize, protect, and grow wealth in a way that lines up with real life. What follows is a high-level look at how that framework works.

Five Pillars of Wealth Creation and Preservation

Why the VAULT Framework

The goal is to provide a simple yet comprehensive system for *both* wealth creation *and* wealth preservation—the two sides of the wealth equation that most financial advice treats separately.

My Authority Position

- NFL experience (high-pressure decision making, team synergy).
- Personal experience (from bankruptcy to wealth creation and money challenges).
- "Standing Guard" philosophy (I protected quarterbacks, now, I protect your money).
- Entrepreneur focus (our target market is entrepreneurs with $1 million-plus in investable assets).
- Track record (uncovered many blind spots in our clients' lives and their testimonials are proof).
  - *Note: Illustrative examples or client testimonials provided may not represent the experience of other clients and are not a guarantee of future performance or success.*

My Professional Focus

Most wealth managers start and end with the money—the "assets under management"—because that's where they make their money. That may leave you exposed. Pro Capital helps you keep it and build it.

V – Vision & Values

- Plan Your Wealth Around 3 Generations–You, Your Children, and Your Grandchildren
- Set Firm Family Money Rules and Values
- Teach Your Children About Money
- Create a Legacy Vision and Family Constitution

Core

Know **why** you want wealth and how you'll create it, then make sure your family also knows.

A – Asset Protection & Acceleration

- Insurance: health, liability, life, umbrella, etc.
- Business Entities: corporations, LLCs, partnerships
- Basic Trust Planning: beneficiary planning, simple revocable trusts
- Legal Documents: estate documents, powers of attorney, wills

Core

This is about building walls around your money so lawsuits and accidents can't take it.

Asset protection plans should be developed and implemented well before problems arise. Due to the fraudulent transfer laws, asset transfers that occur close in proximity to the filing of a lawsuit or bankruptcy can be interpreted by the court as a fraudulent transfer. Proper structuring of these assets is imperative; please seek proper legal and tax advice prior to engaging in re-titling/structuring of any assets. Please note that laws are subject to change and can have an impact on your asset protection strategy.

U – Unshakable Systems

- The "Purpose Driven Investing" Strategy: Allocate Assets with an Eye to "Safe, Predictable Growth"
- Income-First Investing: Assets that Pay You Monthly
- Portfolio Management: Professional Investment Oversight
- Wealth Automation: Systems that Work Without You Watching
- Risk Management: Diversification and Protection Strategies

Core

Make your money work for you so that you don't have to work forever.

L – Lifetimes & Legacies

- Estate Tax Planning: Strategies to Avoid the Forty Percent Death Tax
- Business Succession: Who Runs Your Company When You Can't?
- Advanced Trust Planning: Charitable Trusts, Dynasty Trusts, FLPS, SLATS
- Asset Titling: How Things are Owned for Maximum Protection
- Inheritance Planning: Passing Wealth Without Spoiling Kids

Core

Ensuring that your wealth survives after you're gone.

T – Time & Taxes

- Tax Strategy: Legal Ways to Cut your Tax Bill
- Professional Team Building: Attorneys, CPAS, Financial Advisors All Working Together
- Time Management: Stop Doing $50/Hour Work When You Make $500/Hour
- Process Automation: Systems that Save Time and Money
- Annual Planning: Coordinated Strategy Reviews

Core

This is about keeping more of what you make and getting your time back.

Pro Capital LLC does not offer legal or tax advice. Please consult the appropriate professional regarding your individual circumstance.

Summary

	Financial Planning Focus	Main Goal
V	Family Philosophy	Know your money "why"
A	Basic Protection	Build walls around wealth
U	Investment Strategy	Make money work for you
L	Estate Planning	Wealth survives you
T	Efficiency/Coordination	Keep more, work less

If this fired you up, don't stop here. You've got momentum, use it! Visit www.procapitaltx.com for more information.

Part II
The V.A.U.L.T. Method

Building Wealth That Can't Be Touched, Taken, or Taxed Away

V – Vision & Values

The Legacy Vision Canvas—Planning for 100 Years

Fundamental Ideas:

1. You can't plan your children's lives, but you can plan around their possible mistakes.
2. Even a plan with the best intentions can be a bad plan.
3. Wealth can be generational; be the exception to the rule.

I mentioned two statistics earlier—seventy percent of wealthy families lose their wealth by the second generation; ninety percent lose it by the third.[9] This conclusion, based on a twenty-year-old study of 3,200 families by the Williams Group, begs the question: How can it happen?

Public Domain Illustration, PixelBay.com

---

[9] "Generational Wealth: Why do 70% of Families Lose Their Wealth in the 2nd Generation?" *Nasdaq.com. Op cit.*

The Mitchell Family Story

Imagine a fortune of around $50 million that, in two generations, all but vanished.

Generation One: "Robert Mitchell," an entrepreneur, founded and built a software company, then sold it and retired with $50 million not too many years ago. He was a classic first-generation wealth creator. He worked eighty hours a week, missing family dinners and sacrificing everything to build his dream for his family.

His vision was simple, "I never want my kids to struggle like I did." His fatal assumption was equally simple, "Money solves everything. If I just leave them enough, they'll be set for life." In theory, that sounds perfectly reasonable, but in reality, it usually goes the other way.

Generation Two enters the picture: first child "Sarah" and second child "Michael." The only thing they knew was a life of plenty and, therefore, they never developed an understanding of the effort needed to create and maintain that lifestyle. Sarah was old enough to see some of her dad's sacrifices and, therefore, understood the value of hard work though she never experienced day-to-day struggle. Michael didn't see his father's struggle and didn't have a dad around to teach him how to deal with problems. So when the usual troubles of life hit him, he learned to avoid them with drugs. Happily, in his twenties, he realized his problem and cleaned up his act.

The Problem

When Dad passed, Sarah (now in her late thirties) received a $15 million inheritance. She made reasonable initial decisions, bought a modest home, invested conservatively, and continued working as a teacher. Michael became another addiction tragedy. Based on his years of sobriety, he received a lump sum $3 million bequest. Sadly, he fell off the wagon, as they say. He went right back to the same dose level that he was using fifteen years previous. In a matter of months after receiving this inheritance, he suffered a fatal overdose. His body simply couldn't handle the drug levels he'd built up to in his previous addiction cycle. He left behind a wife and two kids.

Now, we have a family completely torn apart by guilt and blame as they try to sort out their son's and brother's death. We also have someone with a good heart who misdirects that guilt into a tragedy of a completely different sort.

Sarah devastated by her brother's death, decides to do something meaningful. She creates a foundation with $8 million—over half of her remaining inheritance. Her noble intention hopes to create a lasting impact for underprivileged children that might prevent other senseless drug tragedies.

I should make it clear that this was a better plan than other extreme examples, I could mention. Cornelius Vanderbilt's family lost $400 billion (that's an estimate adjusted for inflation) in just three generations through lavish consumption—mansions, parties, and other ego trips. (Yes, I'm being kind. They didn't lose anything; they flat-out wasted it!) Sarah's foundation wasn't lavish consumption, but it became equally destructive to generational wealth. Within five years, the foundation had burned through the entire $8 million. Her remaining wealth dwindled down to $4.2 million after taxes, living expenses, and some poor investments.

Generation Three enters the picture. These inheritors, born in the early 21st Century, will probably inherit around $1.5 million each. Overall, that means close to ninety percent of the wealth their grandfather created is gone—never to be recovered.

The Solution

Michael got his inheritance based on a false assumption: that he would stay clean and sober. When the plan was created, the attorney (a friend of mine) asked Robert, "What's the distribution plan for your money—an outright transfer or a graduated sequence?"

An outright distribution, as the word implies, transfers all the inheritance as soon as practical after the passing. A graduated distribution transfers incrementally, let's say, each child gets a third on their 21st birthday, another third at thirty, and the rest at forty. Those two options comprise almost a hundred percent of the documents our firm reviews from prospects and new clients—and both are bad ideas.

I've been very frank with some clients. I set them up with what they want because, ultimately, I'm paid to do what the client wants, but I'm also paid for my expertise and experience. Both warn me what can happen in these situations.

For Michael, the lump-sum decision was made after a long conversation with the attorney. He advised that, because of Michael's drug history, they put in parameters in place. A third-party custodian could manage the assets for him. To receive any distribution of his inheritance, he'd have to prove employment and sobriety—the ability to handle the money in an adult fashion. The family said no; they trusted him—a bad call on their part. History proved that he was not ready, but he'd been sober for so long that they felt they should give him a vote of confidence. They assumed the past equaled the future—an emotional decision.

Sarah, like so many NFL players I saw, had a good heart initially but executed poorly. A lot of NFL players come from situations or stories that were foundational to their success. The most successful entrepreneurs we work with often had something devastating that helped them build. Like Sarah, many want to give back. There are also tax advantages, but that's logical thinking which usually comes later. Note this: our decisions are mainly emotional, with bots of logic. We have to know this to control our decision-making. The problem is, without counsel, you can blow through money fast. A friend of mine, who spent twenty years on boards of various non-profits, is fond of reminding people two very important—and somewhat counter-intuitive—facts:

1. There's no such thing as a not-for-profit business. If you don't take in more money than you spend, you will go out of business.
2. There are as many forms of profit as there are enterprises. Define your profit carefully because earning that profit is how you get people to give you their hard-earned money.

Sarah's guilt led her to make emotional decisions. Her $8 million could've been the basis for a very successful organization impacting many children and their families. Sarah failed to create an endowment structure, forcing them to spend principal instead of earnings. That's about as common a mistake as you can find. Their inexperienced board failed to provide proper oversight, failed to audit administrative costs, and failed to develop a sustainable development (fundraising) strategy.

Donations to your church, to local youth groups, to historical or arts societies, or any of a thousand other groups is a great idea. It has solid tax benefits, sets an example for others, and creates profit for the community. But, if the leaders aren't good with money, if the board doesn't understand their oversight obligation and demand quality management, and if the funding isn't set up to promote long-term survival and growth, then all the good hearts and good intentions in the world won't bring success—they'll guarantee failure.

The Other Problem

Many parents don't discuss money with their kids (their second-generation heirs) or their grandkids (their third-generation heirs). Instead, they work to give them everything they didn't have as children. Not a bad plan on its own but, by doing this, they unintentionally cheat their kids—who may grow up not understanding the value of money. There was an attorney, a specialist in retirement planning, who said he'd never met a trust fund kid who was worth anything. I can't go that far, but I've seen some pretty spoiled kids come from amazing people. I've also seen amazing wealthy people raise great kids. The point is that we have to be intentional about bringing our kids and grandkids into the mix when it comes to money.

Families, both those with tremendous wealth and those with just enough, often neglect to create a plan at all. Many who do have such a plan don't let their heirs take part in it. If you own a business, who's taking over? Do they want to? Can they run it? Who gets the house? Same questions. Who gets the stocks, bonds, and other financial instruments? Same questions. Will charities be supported? Will your children get anything? That's a legitimate option, by the way—you can require your children earn their own way entirely, with all your heirs being charities.

The Other Solution

A solid financial position is one of those things that's worth fighting for. The tragedies come when we stop fighting. A couple of stories:

How many of us know someone who doesn't have a close relationship with family members? One guy I know has never married, but he thinks he's made a good effort. In fact, he's still out there working to start a family, even though his siblings are now grandparents. At the same time, he feels that no one in his family ever fought to maintain a relationship with him. When he went off to college, "They just let me go." Decades of estrangement followed, with little communication and less contact. It was almost as if they were glad he was gone.

When I heard that story, I immediately thought of relationships in which someone just needs an advocate or a little help. A friend I knew ran for a position in our locality. Somebody else loved spewing political garbage in the media and posted a recent picture of my friend with an old story about a petty theft charge from when he was a kid. Technically, that's fair game because it was on his record and available to the public. But I knew the family well, and I didn't think that story was any indicator of the person I knew. So I posted a rebuttal on the town's social media page in response to the story. All I did was encourage people to get to know him. My friend and I became even closer over that and, when he later gave his life to Christ, he asked me to baptize him.

So how is any of this a solution to financial problems?

Capital goes where it is welcome and stays where it is well-treated.
—Walter Wriston, former CEO of Citibank [attr.]

Financial success isn't natural; it doesn't just happen, any more than a healthy relationship with relatives or friends just happens. You need to work to create healthy money habits for your children and grandchildren, just as you work to maintain a healthy personal relationship. In the old days, parents brought their kids to work. The kids would learn a trade and how to keep a home. Boys learned how to be men from their fathers, and girls learned how to be women from their mothers. Financial success with our children isn't as complicated as you think. You just have to bring them along for the ride and be patient enough to teach and answer their questions.

Steven Covey, in his famous book, *Seven Habits of Highly Effective People*, wrote:

Habit 1: Be Proactive.

Habit 2: Begin with the End in Mind.[10]

In our Vision & Values meeting—my first planning meeting with new clients—I ask them, "What do you want this life to look like? What do you want out of your business? What do you want it to produce?" We're trying to protect this thing but in order to foresee and prepare against threats, we

---

[10] Steven Covey, *The 7 Habits of Highly Effective People*. New York City: Free Press (an imprint of Simon & Schuster), 1989. Quoted at https://www.franklincovey.com/courses/the-7-habits/

need to know where you're headed so we can identify those threats. In essence, what do you want your money to do for you? From this first discussion, we create the "Legacy Vision Canvas"—a one-page family wealth blueprint.

There's an old joke, "If you don't know where you're going, you'll probably end up someplace else."

Frankly, history has proven to me that it's no joke. Most of those unintended destinations are places you don't want to be.

I don't think I can repeat it too often or overemphasize it: wealth *creation* and wealth *preservation*. Which leads to Walter Wriston's other famous attribution:

> Information about money has become almost as important as money itself.

In order to accomplish those goals, we need to define, very specifically, what the word *wealth* means to you. It might be $10 million in the bank so you can retire and never worry about money again. (More on that in Chapter 7.) It might be leaving a paycheck-employee status and becoming an entrepreneur. It might be having enough money to get your children through college and give them a debt-free start in adulthood. It might be a hundred other things. Only you and your spouse can answer that question. Once the goals are defined, we can reverse-engineer a way to create that wealth.

In doing that, we gather information—the more, the better. Anything might affect your wealth creation and preservation plan. Some affects we welcome; others we dread.

In our story, Robert, the original creator of the wealth, never articulated why he was building wealth beyond "so my kids don't struggle." For the record, kids should struggle. They need to learn to overcome challenges because nobody gets off free, and Mom and Dad are not always going to be around to clean up the resulting mess. If it isn't money, it's health problems or marital problems or business problems or legal problems or whatever else arises. No one goes through life without a disaster or two—or three.

Robert didn't have a three-generation vision. Because of his lack of planning, each generation made decisions based on their immediate circumstances. That meant emotion-based decisions instead of choices grounded on goals and financial literacy. This is how we avoid being driven by emotion. Too many families don't discuss money, which leads to heirs who don't understand how to handle it properly. Robert avoided those conversations because they made him uncomfortable. This is horrifyingly common, and the disastrous results are all around us.

As I write this, we just had a Vision & Values conversation with a new client couple. This husband and wife (mid-forties with children) have a great foundation in what they've created thus far. But they're looking at potentially taking care of their aging parents and some siblings who are destructive in their own way. On the upside, they have an uncle who's been really successful, creating a $10 million-plus estate. The husband will be a beneficiary of that estate.

I asked them questions—her about her parents and him about his and anyone else who's involved. I challenged them to have financial conversations with their parents and uncle, then come back and report. Both reported that the conversations went badly.

She said, "Mom is an artist. She doesn't want to talk about it. She's in charge of the finances. Dad just kind of skirted the issue, not doing anything. He just expects some money to be there. Mom doesn't want to talk about any of this stuff, even though she's handling the money. She thinks something's wrong when I bring it up. I told her I'm just asking to make sure that we have things in order for you so that it's not in peril when you guys are gone. It ended up basically being a big emotional blowup." His experience wasn't much different.

Their parents' generation is cemented in this cone of silence when it comes to talking about money. For some reason, many are so uncomfortable with this conversation that they just refuse to have it.

What happens now? I don't know anything about their parents' finances, so the plans I'll suggest are subject to all the risks of passing wealth to the next generation with no ability to affect the outcome of that transition because I don't know anything about that wealth. It's especially sad that now, when I'm working with a second generation that's trying to do the smart thing, Mom and Dad aren't being responsible. We're bringing up the right issues, but the parents aren't allowing a resolution. The children aren't grasping; like in the parable of the Prodigal Son, they're actually being respectful, effectively saying, "Hey, I just want to make sure you're taken care of."

It goes on and on in too many families. Transfer failure—the number three reason for loss of generational wealth—exists because the family fails to identify and deal with risks. Why not? Emotion. Again and again, we come back to emotion.

Remember that repeated line from *The Godfather* movies: "It's not personal; it's just business." Your family finances are your family's business. You have receipts, expenditures, taxes, deductions, investments, inventory. You have to treat it like a business. You have to make decisions—some of them tough decisions—and you have to make the right decisions, or the business goes under. You need a business plan.

The Legacy Vision Canvas

Let's take another look at the Mitchell family.

They failed to identify and transfer the obvious risk—addiction. They should've used a structured trust with sobriety requirements. The subsequent charitable risk should have been met with an endowment component, not a spend down model.

What if the Mitchell family had used the VAULT Method Vision & Value framework as a practical planning tool? First, we ask, "What do we want our wealth to accomplish seventy-five years from now?"

- Generation One is the builders; they want to create a sustainable wealth engine.
- Generation Two is the stewards; they want to preserve and grow the fortune while learning what their responsibilities entail.
- Generation Three is the impact-makers; they use the accumulated wealth to provide for the family and make an impact on society.

Second, we establish the family values—core standards that guide all financial decisions, non-negotiable principles, and a consequence framework for values violations.

Third, we create a risk-transfer matrix for each generation. We identify specific risks, then create mechanisms, such as a structured trust, to minimize the impacts of those risks.

Fourth, we create a generational education roadmap. We set out an age-appropriate financial literacy curriculum, including values-based decision-making frameworks, mentorship, and accountability systems.

Fifth, we list trigger-event protocols—pre-planned responses to specific incidents. This is a big one for us as we deal with predictable challenges: death of the patriarch or matriarch, addiction, relapse, divorce, business failure, economic crisis, and others.

All of this reimagines Robert's family and shows how their Legacy Vision Canvas would have changed everything. Using the VAULT Method, Michael, instead of inheriting a $3 million lump sum, could have received an annual distribution for his family's basic needs. Bonus distributions could have been made when he demonstrated continued sobriety milestones. Full access to his funds would have been granted when all the boxes were checked and he had truly proven he was capable of handling that responsibility. The bottom line: Michael would still be alive. His fortune would still have $3 million or more; his wife would still have her husband, and the children would still have their father.

Sarah's charitable-giving instinct would probably have kicked in eventually. Instead of an emotional $8 million foundation blowout, we would have had a $2 million endowment generating $100,000 annually in perpetuity. We would have had family involvement in grant-making decisions and professional foundation management, resulting in meaningful impact forever instead of a five-year burnout.

Generation Three, instead of a $1.5 million bequest per heir, would inherit $12-15 million in properly preserved wealth. Strong family values would have been established; real financial literacy would have become one of the family values. Unity and shared purpose within the family would have been strengthened with a tradition of financial stability.

The total result of this process, which sounds complex but it really isn't, is true generational wealth with character and purpose. Literally a win-win-win scenario—for each individual, for the family, and for the community.

And the best part? It all starts with an easy thirty-minute interview to complete this exercise. This is not a "proud papa" exaggeration, but my children (Grace, 10, and Hank, 5) are already able to understand some of this. I've created a certain amount of wealth, as has Megan, a lawyer. We're the Generation One wealth creators. Nowhere near $50 million yet but like all good parents, we don't want our kids to struggle or go through the things that we went through. So we teach them what they can understand—and, for the record, children often understand more than we give them credit for.

I also have this burning desire to leave an incredible legacy, one that outlasts me long after I'm gone. I want my children to understand the powerful lessons I've learned from all the people we've served. It's reiterated over and over with our clients and others I've met. We're on the right track—one that you can be on as well.

Your V.A.U.L.T. Vision Canvas™ Worksheet

Take 30 minutes right now to complete this exercise.

1. Your 3-Generation Vision (complete this sentence):

Seventy-five years from now, I want my family's wealth to have accomplished:

Generation 1 (You): ______________________________

Generation 2 (Children): ______________________________

Generation 3 (Grandchildren): ______________________________

2. Your Non-Negotiable Family Values:

List down three to five core values that should guide **all** of your family's financial decisions.

1. ______________________________

2. ______________________________

3. ______________________________

4. ______________________________

5 ______________________________

3. Your Risk Assessment:

What are the top risks that could destroy your family's wealth and how do you work around them?

1.   TM
____

2.   TM
____

3.   TM
____

4.   TM
____

5.   TM
____

(TM = Transfer mechanism)

4. Your Family's Greatest Vulnerability:

If I died tomorrow, the biggest threat to our wealth would be:

The safeguard I need to put in place is:

____

____

____

____

A Piece of Advice

True wealth isn't measured by *your* bank account—it's measured by *your family's* bank accounts one hundred years from now.

CHAPTER 6

A – Asset Protection & Acceleration

Building Wealth That Can't Be Touched

Fundamental Ideas:

1. Start with insurance.
2. Proper structure of assets.
3. Prepare for circumstances where you are not in control.

Let's Expand on Those a Little

As we look at the layers of protection, insurance is the front-line. Insurance is the ability to pool money with a collection of people to share the risk on any given liability. No one likes paying premiums for something we may never see a return on, but you praise it when you need it. This is key to start.

Your entity structure, generally meaning your limited liability corporation (LLC), segments your assets. This could be for commerce, personal wealth management, or a slew of other reasons. If done correctly, you separate these assets so any liability in one cannot affect the other. An example would be if your business gets sued and the liability from the lawsuit can't reach your personal assets, or vice versa.

A trust can protect your assets by transferring ownership from you (as a person) to the trust, which is a separate legal entity. Depending on the structure, a trust can protect personal assets in much the same way an LLC protects business assets. Since you don't own the assets, it is difficult for creditors to access them. You maintain control over those assets by naming yourself as trustee.

Insurance: Liability, Life, Umbrellas, and More

The first layer is the most common, although even our best clients have all come in severely underinsured (or had none at all). I've already mentioned the one-beer nightmare. In that case, the insurance company voided coverage because there was a minor with alcohol in her system. When I was in my accident in high school, I lost my car insurance because I had two violations: speeding and an accident. Insurance is a contract, and you're required to comply with all the rules that the insurance company sets. There is not a whole lot of negotiation going on when you buy insurance, but you do get what you pay for. The lower and middle markets largely clamor over price, but a common theme I see in life is *"you get what you pay for."* That means if you shop cheap, you might end up cussing when you have a real problem that needs covering, but you end up paying out of pocket. Once the deal is made and premiums start flowing, the insurer is obligated to cover you in accidents, etc., up to the limit of your coverage. (Remember that last phrase, we'll come back to it.)

Health

Most of us, through our employer, the government, or on our own, have some form of health insurance. After age sixty-five, most of us end up with Medicare—by law, the government signs you up for Medicare when you start collecting Social Security, with premiums automatically deducted from your SSA benefits.

Even then, you have decisions to make. Do you need additional disability or long-term care insurance? This gets into the "sandwich generation" discussion. Do your parents have sufficient coverage, and if not, are you going to end up footing the bill or, worse, repeating their mistake? Those of us who still have parents with us and have children have three levels of responsibility. We're responsible for ourselves and our children, but we might also become responsible for our parents. With that in mind, remember the old saying, "Failing to plan is planning to fail."

Today, people live longer, so that elder-care burden can last decades and more and more, our seasoned citizens need professional care. If that can't happen at home, a care facility can cost up to $500,000 per year, depending on the level and number of services provided. Remember, these aren't charity wards; they're for-profit businesses. You might be thrilled to see that they have a staff physician to watch out for Mom and Dad, plus a barber shop/hair salon, a pool, a staff nutritionist planning meals, a van with trips to the movies or the mall, and on and on. All those added services are attractive, but they carry an added price that you'll be paying, and they are not cheap.

Medically necessary costs could be covered by long-term care insurance, but the frills will most likely have to be covered by your parents' personal retirement funds or their children's paychecks.

A mentor of mine once suggested that I write liability waivers for my business. I took her advice because she had far more experience than I had, and I soon found out it was sound advice. A husband and wife came in, and when I explained long-term care to them, he disregarded it. "Long-term care is a scam," he said. And I said, "Okay, here's my waiver. It states that I explained the benefits of long-term care as I knew them, and you declined that coverage."

Well, the following year, his mental health went south, and he became abusive toward his wife. She had to put him in a home, unable to live with his deteriorating mental state. You can imagine what that did to their financial position.

By the way, my mentor also had a general rule of thumb: anybody with $10 million in investable assets was considered self-insured. I adopted her rule and later took on a client who owned a string of senior living facilities. When I mentioned $10 million as a general number for self-insurance, she actually laughed at me. A little unsure, I asked, "What's so funny?"

"Oh," she replied, "I've seen estates way bigger than that get eaten up by this business." You can imagine I was surprised. So now, it's a normal part of the plan, especially since you can leverage thirty-three cents on the dollar and leave it to your estate if it goes unused.

Liability

Have you ever had those times in your life where you were driving a little carefree? You were jamming the tunes a little loud, having a great time, and then you had to hit the brakes all of a sudden to avoid hitting the person in front of you? Yeah, me too. You spend the rest of the drive with the radio off and your hands at ten and two, being extra cautious.

Liability, as a general term, includes homeowners' insurance that covers accidents that happen on your property, auto insurance for accidents involving your car or someone else's, and general liability (an "umbrella policy") insurance over and above your other policies.

A quick search in August 2025 showed that a $1 million general liability insurance policy could cost as little as $50 to $100 per month. Over a forty-year working life, even allowing for inflation, that's roughly $100,000 in total premiums. That's pennies on the dollar compared to other insurances. And well worth it if you need it. Depending on your net worth and structure, you could need much more than $1 million—not just because you require more, but because $1 million is basically a rounding error for an insurance company and that'll give you the C-team legal representation from the insurance company.

So, like I've asked previously: if you were in a car accident and someone sued for $30 million, where's the other $29 million coming from?

Life

I was listening to the radio one day, and I was surprised to hear someone I respect suggest that a couple with a $2 million life insurance policy was adequately covered. If the husband dies, said that pundit, the wife has $2 million to take care of her for the rest of her life. General statements like that should never be taken seriously. Every family is different, every situation is different, every plan has to reflect those differences.

Let me ask a few questions:

- Is the widow an empty-nester, or does she have children at home? Are the children in stable marriages, or might she have to take over raising some grandchildren?
- Is this the only marriage? Did he have children (and grandchildren) from previous unions? Was his split from previous spouse(s) amicable, or is this one last chance for revenge?
- Is anyone going to contest the will?
- Was he the only source of household income, or did she have her own? Did he have Social Security benefits, employment pensions, IRAs, investments, a stock portfolio, or other sources that she can tap into?
- Is their house paid off? Do they have debts? Are there ongoing business interests, contracts, etc., that need to be settled?
- How old is she? How's her health? How long will she live? What health problems will she have to deal with?
- What lifestyle did the couple enjoy? I know a lady about my age who pulls down $4 million per year and threw her daughter a $300,000 wedding. She and her husband have $1 million each in life insurance. Do you think that was adequate to maintain their lifestyle?

Suddenly, $2 million isn't looking like such a great fortune. In fact, as I was discussing this with my writing coach, he started laughing. When I asked why, he said, "I just figured something out."

He's almost twenty-five years older than me, born near the end of the baby boom, while I'm near the front of Gen Y, a "Millennial." He watched the moon landing live and celebrated the USA's bicentennial. His mom drove a station wagon instead of a minivan and filled up the gas tank for $5.00. He bought bread for 50¢ a loaf and paid about $1,500 for tuition, books, dorm room, and everything else during his first year of college. I still didn't get why he was laughing.

"Because we're still thinking about 'big money' in terms of the 1950s and 1960s!"

He was right, sixty or seventy years ago, $1 million was a real fortune—you could retire very happily. Well, if you listen to insurance ads on TV or radio, *that's still the number they advertise as a great policy payout*. Here's the thing:

Today, $100,000 per year is a solid, middle-class income, but it's not rich. (He told me his dad was middle class, making $20,000 per year when he was a kid.) Today, a million-dollar life insurance is equal to ten years of middle-class income. That's gross, not net; you still have to deal with taxes, inflation, and every other challenge I already listed, and they add up fast! The US Federal Reserve Bank has a goal of keeping inflation at two percent per year when averaged over the long haul. I've got about twenty years until sixty-five, the traditional retirement age. If we meet the Fed's goal, two percent inflation over twenty years totals just short of fifty percent, meaning whatever a $100,000 income could buy in 2025 will cost around $148,600 in 2045.

And your million-dollar policy payment ran out a decade ago.

The Bottom Line

Many of us, maybe most, are dangerously–potentially tragically–underinsured across the board.

A good rule of thumb is four percent. That's the average interest or dividends that good investments will return over the long haul. So, if I want that $100,000 income, I need to divide it by four percent (that is, multiply it by twenty-five), and I get $2.5 million.

With a $2.5 million insurance payout, statistically speaking, if I'm pulling four percent off my portfolio, I have better than a ninety percent chance of not running out of money ever. But, again, inflation isn't steady, but it is cumulative, so anything extra that you can save over that is icing on the cake.

The goal is to preserve necessary income that serves the surviving spouse and children–to make sure they can last financially and take plenty of time to grieve while not spending principal–the money that would have earned you interest or dividends in the future.

Business Entities

LLCs, The Corporate Wall

Regarding the second layer, I won't say that everybody should have an LLC, because a lot of people can't use them. It's a business, and you have to conduct business to be legitimate. The IRS takes a dim view of people who dodge their taxes.

That said, having an LLC, a corporation, or a partnership is vital, under certain circumstances, to properly safeguard your assets–and even more so as your assets grow.

In Texas and, I assume, in other states, an LLC is easy to create. You can get standardized forms online, and most people can figure them out in an afternoon. Many law firms will do the paperwork for you neatly and inexpensively. When I first filed, my business wasn't worth much of anything, so I only paid the $300 filing fee to the Secretary of the State of Texas and got it all done online. The website of your Secretary of State should have all the answers to your questions.

Please note that the Secretary of State doesn't require you to file all documents with them; you just have to file a registration form. In addition, you'll need an operating agreement—the equivalent of an employment contract—between you and your company. That's the most common culprit for problems. Either someone never creates it, or they never update it. So, do your due diligence, make sure you have all your documents in place, keep hard and electronic copies, and update them on a consistent basis. If you don't, you can potentially lose your veil of protection.

With an LLC that doesn't have all its ducks in a row, a good lawyer (good for whoever is suing you, that is) can pierce the veil. If I were a litigating attorney suing an LLC, I can claim that it's not a real company if I see their paperwork is sloppy or missing, or if the business co-mingles assets with the person. That's often a winning strategy.

If you organized an LLC with a stated purpose of buying and selling real estate, but you've since changed careers and you're now operating as a marketing business, they may have a case. They can claim the business isn't real. If, as litigator, I can provide a good enough case, the judge can say, "Well, you got a point, it's not what it claims to be. All right, I'm going to strike that LLC from the record and include business with personal assets."

It happens, but only to wild ducks—so keep those little quackers in their row.

Trusts

The third layer (we've also touched on this already) is a basic revocable living trust. This entity is designed to avoid probate and the potential contests that people could bring against your estate.

When you transfer assets to a trust, the trust becomes the legal owner of that property. You control that property as trustee. In establishing a trusteeship, you also name a successor in case of death, resignation, or removal of the original trustee, and specify under what circumstances those things could happen. That way, when you die, nothing happens to the trust or what's in it; they simply—and immediately—come under the control of the successor trustee.

Once again, it's the proper listing of assets and proper funding of that estate plan (meaning creating the right documents) that ensures the inheritance gets passed on intact to the deserving heirs.

Advance Healthcare Directives

The fourth and final layer covers your final wishes. Each state, by statute, defines the terms of a directive. Most require one or two witnesses or a notary public for the directive to be enforceable. You can easily find this information online. Online forms are also available, or any lawyer who deals with trusts and other similar matters can draft one for you. Many package these forms together as a group.

Remember, you can experience accidents, illnesses, or other serious situations at any age. These advance directives aren't just for seasoned citizens. Every adult needs to prepare these documents.

Living Will

It specifies to your family and healthcare providers what kinds of medical treatment you accept or refuse if you are unable to communicate personally or have been incapacitated in some way. In most states, a living will is in effect only if you meet specific medical criteria that render you unable to communicate your wishes.

One specific, very common type of short living will is the "do not resuscitate" order, or DNR. You don't need a full living will to have a DNR or a "do not intubate" (DNI) order. You can simply tell your healthcare providers and have it noted on your chart. If you have a written DNR or DNI, keep a copy at home, in case questions arise later. It's better to have the full documents signed, sealed, and delivered to avoid any confusion.

Medical Power of Attorney

This document assigns authority to make medical decisions, including end-of-life care, to a specific person. Called by various names, including healthcare agent, proxy, surrogate, representative, attorney-in-fact or simply the patient advocate, he or she is a family member or friend you trust to make healthcare decisions for you when you cannot. The document should include specific directions to the proxy covering the full range of care you will accept, and alternates in case the primary is unavailable. Always have a clear and detailed discussion with your proxy regarding your wishes.

Beyond the obvious (an agent must be of legal age), your state law may have other requirements. They're listed online on numerous websites.

Word to the Wise

Tell your primary care physician of your living will, DNR, power-of-attorney, and so on. Inform other care providers every time you stay at a hospital or healthcare facility. At the very least, if needed, we keep it on record in our VAULT so that you can access it quickly. An ancient Roman teacher once said, "We should not write so we *can be understood*, we should write so we *cannot be misunderstood*."

(That's good advice in every aspect of life.)

CHAPTER 7

U – Unshakeable Systems

Making Your Investments Work So You Don't Have To

Fundamental Ideas:

1. It's never about gross sales; it's about net cashflow.
2. True wealth is not measured in assets; it's measured in usable income. Cash on hand pays bills.
3. Growing our wealth isn't the goal—it's the method. Protecting what we've grown is the goal.

This leads to two serious problems:

1. Fear and greed are the dominant factors that create emotional decision-making, and Wall Street knows this.
2. Wall Street plays on both to sell the next "hot" stock or product, even though they haven't considered (and really don't care about) your needs or desires.

We begin by sharing some fundamental ideas that Wall Street (and money managers in general) have preached forever:

Section 1: Wall Street's Four Most Dangerous Ideas

1. The Market Always Goes up in the Long-Term

The phrase "the market always goes up" is a Wall Street mantra. While it's fundamentally true over the long haul, it's also dangerously misleading. If you zoom out across nearly a century, the US stock market has produced annualized returns close to eleven percent. Markets, however, don't move in straight lines; they travel a jagged road like the silhouette of a mountain range, filled with booms and busts, bears and bulls, deep crashes, stagnation periods, and sharp recoveries.

Downturns can devastate people who need money when that downturn happens.

Chart: S&P 500 Index at Inflection Points[11]

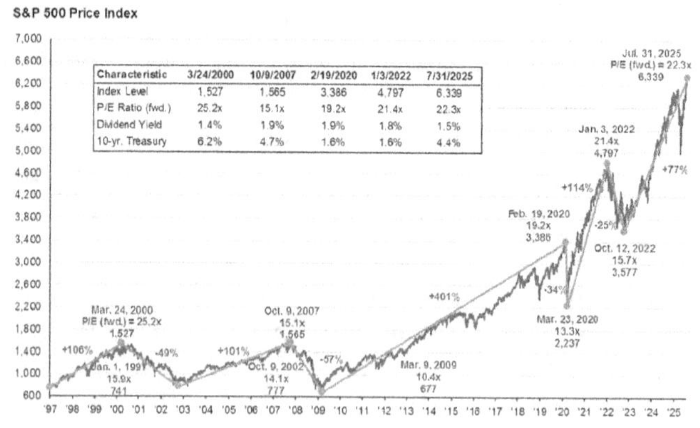

Characteristic	3/24/2000	10/9/2007	2/19/2020	1/3/2022	7/31/2025
Index Level	1,527	1,565	3,386	4,797	6,339
P/E Ratio (fwd.)	25.2x	15.1x	19.2x	21.4x	22.3x
Dividend Yield	1.4%	1.9%	1.9%	1.8%	1.5%
10-yr. Treasury	6.2%	4.7%	1.6%	1.6%	4.4%

[11] Unbylined, "Guide to the Markets," *JPMorgan.com*. New York City: J.P. Morgan Chase & Co., 31 August 2025 (page 4). https://am.jpmorgan.com/us/en/asset-management/adv/insights/market-insights/guide-to-the-markets/

The Standard & Poor's 500 (S&P 500) is an unmanaged group of securities considered to be representative of the stock market in general. It is a market-value-weighted index, with each stock's weight in the index proportionate to its market value. You cannot invest directly into an index. Past performance is not a guarantee of future results.

The S&P 500 is an "index"—a yardstick that helps indicate market trends. A rising index means a healthier economy. Look carefully at the green line. In 1997, it passed 700 and rose to 1500 in 2000. Then the dot-com crash hit, and the S&P 500 fell almost fifty percent from 2000 to 2002. The index rose again until late 2007, when the housing bubble burst, creating an even bigger loss of fifty-seven percent. The market rebounded, heading upward in 2009, but didn't fully recover (reach 1500 again) until 2013, a dozen years after the first crash. Many investors who retired during that time (having put all their eggs in the Wall Street basket) found themselves selling investments at losses to pay bills. It was a bad decade and a half for anyone who retired. More deep dips occurred in 2020, 2022, and 2025 but, fortunately, were not as devastating, being briefer and shallower. Maybe the next one won't be either.

For people pulling money from portfolios for retirement or business owners relying on portfolios as backup cash, the "always goes up" myth creates false confidence. US stock markets have risen overall during the last one hundred years, but few people even live one hundred years. Traditionally, we work about forty years, looking to retire at sixty-five or seventy years, and hoping to live comfortably for a decade or two or three on what we squirreled away.

During the tech bubble of the late 1990s, many entrepreneurs saw sky-high valuations for their companies. Venture capital money flowed easily, IPOs skyrocketed, and growth seemed unstoppable. But when that tech bubble burst (in the "dot-com crash"), startups collapsed suddenly, even those who had raised millions in venture capital. Entrepreneurs who counted on the myth to exit with a rich payoff or to fund further growth suddenly found themselves locked out of capital markets for nearly a decade. Bad timing killed their liquidity.

Real-World Analogy

It's like planting an apple tree. People say, "Trees always grow taller." That's true—if a storm doesn't knock it down before you get any apples. If it does, you're left hungry. You can always plant another tree—the market will rise again—but that doesn't help when you need food today.

2. Diversification Helps Protect You

For decades, diversification was treated like gospel. By spreading money across different asset classes—stocks, bonds, international markets—you were supposed to reduce risk. The classic formula was the 60/40 portfolio: sixty percent stocks, forty percent bonds. It worked well in normal times because stocks and bonds tended to move in opposite directions. When stocks fell, bonds provided a buffer.

But diversification is no magic shield. In 2022, stocks fell nineteen percent and bonds lost thirteen percent, leaving the 60/40 portfolio down sixteen percent overall, its worst year since 1937. Investors learned that diversification into just two or three types of financial instruments doesn't protect you during a system-wide shock. When inflation spikes, interest rates rise and when a global crisis hits, correlations converge—meaning everything falls together. You're left exposed, even when you think you're balanced.

Traditional diversification is useful but not bulletproof. Full diversification spreads risk among assets with fundamentally different risk drivers. That means real estate, precious metals, alternatives, private credit, structured insurance, and more. These are not different shades of the same color—this is the full spectrum of investment opportunities, where each carries a completely different set of pros and cons.

For entrepreneurs, this mirrors what happened to restaurants during COVID. Owners thought they were diversified because they had multiple menu items or locations. But when in-person dining shut down across America, all those revenue streams evaporated at once. The only restaurants that survived were those who had true diversification—online ordering, take out, home delivery, catering, or strong cash reserves. Like the 60/40 portfolio, "diversified" wasn't really diversified against system-wide shocks.

Real-World Analogy

It's the classic "Don't put all your eggs in one basket" scenario. If the neighbor's dogs get into the coop and kill the chickens, your egg supply ends regardless of how many baskets you had. Exactly that happened in 2022—the stock and bond markets sank together.

3. Big Financial Firms Mean Safety

By now, everybody's heard the phrase, "too big to fail." Nothing is too big to fail. Even the mighty Mongol Empire, the largest government in known history, fell apart when the circumstances favored their enemies. Investors often assume that big firms mean safety. If their money is with a house-hold name—on a glossy statement or in a skyscraper office—they feel reassured. (A reasonable assumption, because they didn't get to be that big by being stupid.) Sadly, once they get that big, like a successful individual, ego can outstrip intelligence, and everybody makes mistakes. The 2008 financial crisis proved that even the largest, most prestigious firms can make big mistakes.

Lehman Brothers, a 158-year-old bank, went bankrupt overnight. Their stock price fell from $133 in 2007 to $10 in 2008. Its bankruptcy triggered a 4.5 percent drop in the Dow in a single day—the largest since 9/11.

Bear Stearns, once a titan of Wall Street, was sold for pennies on the dollar. AIG, one of the largest insurers in the world, required a massive government bailout. Merrill Lynch, a 105-year-old broker, was bought out by Bank of America in an all-stock deal. These weren't unknown players—they were Wall Street institutions. Yet their size and brand offered no insulation when they miscalculated the markets.

The Other Side of the Coin

I can't tell you how many times people come to me saying, "I think I just hit a cap with my financial advisor/firm. They don't have any more to offer my family." This is true because no financial advisor can know it all; the system is just too complex. So, like many other industries, we specialize. Our firm deals with clients having $1 million-plus in investable assets. We create specialized solutions for problems that regularly arise among that group of people, and we believe we've become very good at it. A small-investor specialist might deal mostly with young individuals and couples who need help paying off student loans, buying their first house, and starting a stock portfolio. That's just as valuable to that market segment as we are to ours.

So, find an advisor and firm who understand your situation and can customize your plan to fit your needs and goals. Then, don't feel too much loyalty. When you outgrow your advisor, find a new professional. This is closely related to the "too big to fail" idea.

Never confuse brand trust with financial security.

Big firms have vast infrastructures and distribution, but they can't guarantee outcomes any more than I can. No one can predict with certainty how the markets will react because we don't know what will happen tomorrow. We know what happened in the past, and we see today's trends; however, in the end, the only true safety comes from a sound preparation and a good plan: liquidity buffers, income planning, and risk management—not the logo on the statement.

Small business owners learned this lesson when Toys "R" Us went bankrupt in 2017. Hundreds of toy manufacturers lost their biggest distributor overnight. They thought they were safe because they partnered with a "too big to fail" retailer. But Toys "R" Us's collapse revealed how dangerous it is to tie your business to the stability of one big partner. Just like Lehman, big names don't equal safety.

Real-World Analogy

Flying (Superman keeps reminding us) is, statistically, still the safest way to travel. Well, remember Flight 1549, the plane that ditched in the Hudson River in 2009? That Airbus A320 was built by the best aircraft manufacturer in Europe. US Airways had seventy years of safe operations. Pilots

Chesley "Sully" Sullenberger and Jeffrey Skiles had over 35,000 hours of inflight experience between them.

A flock of Canadian geese overruled all that excellence in about five seconds.

4. Net Worth Determines Your Lifestyle

A 2022 Northwestern Mutual study found that thirty-seven percent of retirees worry about outliving their savings—even those with a high net worth. Net worth does not automatically secure a lifestyle. We discussed this somewhat in a previous chapter.

In our culture, net worth is seen as the scoreboard of success. To a point, it is, but it's only one measure. People assume the higher the number, the safer and more comfortable the lifestyle.

Net worth is not income, and your income pays your bills.

A big balance sheet doesn't guarantee a big cash flow.

In 2022, retirees with $2 million in a traditional 60/40 portfolio saw it fall by twenty-one percent after losses and withdrawals. On paper, they still had a high net worth, but their lifestyle security was shaken. Even worse, if you had an all-equity portfolio and the market cut by half, would you be able to cut your income by half and maintain the lifestyle you have now? Not usually. Net worth fluctuates with markets, while lifestyle depends on reliable cash flow.

Entrepreneurs face the same trap. A company may be valued at $10 million, but if it doesn't produce sufficient income, the owner may feel broke. The most famous example is

WeWork, once valued at $47 billion. Its founder was (on paper) a billionaire. The company, however, produced no sustainable income, so when the valuation collapsed, the wealth's true nature was revealed—it was just an illusion. High net worth didn't equal lifestyle stability.

Many business owners fall into this trap when they reinvest everything into growth while failing to secure a personal income stream. They may look wealthy because their business is worth a lot of money, theoretically, but if a downturn hits and they can't pull out the cash they need, their lifestyle suffers.

Liquidity and income determine security.

Real-World Analogy

Imagine having a safe filled with gold coins. They are beautifully shiny, but if you can't buy dinner with one, the practical value is $0.00.

The State of Utah figured a way to work around that problem. In 2011, they passed the Legal Tender Act, which made gold and silver legal tender in the Beehive State—as legal as the greenbacks in our wallets. Still, even 1/20th ounce of gold (the smallest coins anyone made at that time) was worth more than a dinner at most restaurants. There was no practical avenue to use that wealth.

Seeing an opportunity, a private commercial company took thin sheets of gold—1/1,000th of an ounce—and sealed them in plastic sleeves, along with 5-, 10-, 20-, and 50-thousandths of an ounce. These "Goldbacks" are now accepted by over 600 businesses in Utah, with more being added all the time. Several other states have followed Utah's lead.

That Utah law, by the way, specifically prohibits companies from demanding payment in gold and consumers from forcing businesses to accept it. The Legal Tender Act created one more option—one that made the impractical practical.

Practical—spendable—money is the cornerstone of lifestyle.

All the stocks, bonds, homes, commercial office buildings, or whatnots you own have no real-world value unless you can take money out of them and fill up your gas tank.

Section 2: Designing an Unshakable System

Step 1: Calculate Actual Income Needs

- List your monthly budget and multiply by twelve to determine your annual income goal.
- For example: if your budget is $15,000/month, you want a total income of $180,000 per year.

Step 2: Identify Guaranteed Income Sources

- Social Security: $ ___________________.
- Pensions: $ ___________________.
- Others: $ ___________________.
- Total: $ ___________________.
- Subtract Budget: $ ___________________.
- Gap to Fill: $ ___________________.

Step 3: Allocate Assets Using the "SPG" Strategy

My belief is that all investments should produce income now or at some point in the future. I jokingly call it the "Salt, Pepper, Garlic" strategy, but it stands for "Safe, Predictable, or Guaranteed." It's like cooking at home; it works with many dishes. Divide your investments into three categories:

- SPG: these investments must provide liquidity and stable income *not* subject to market drops.
- Hybrid: these investments provide income that fluctuates like a preferred stock.
- Growth: these investments don't provide income today but should at some point in the future.

Step 4: Systematize Everything

Automation is the anti-emotional protection system.

Automation is a logical process. Automatic investing, automatic rebalancing, scheduled income distribution, scheduled professional oversight, and annual reviews and adjustments are a few of the tools that prevent bad decision-making by forcing us to think before we act.

Systemized rules mean we hear scary news, but we don't react; we continue acting according to our preset values and rules.

Logic dominates emotion.

- Establish a predefined investment policy in the family constitution.

- Automatic systems prevent panic selling and other knee-jerk reactions.
- Clear income objectives, set on paper and known to all concerned, guide wiser decisions.
- Demand professional accountability of all professionals involved.

Section 3: Purpose-Driven Investing

With a systematic design in place, we can plan two investment objectives:

- A stable cash flow for current and future expenses.
- Growth designed to beat inflation over time.

Every investment should have a goal of producing income now or at some point in the future.

Step 1: Define Your Objectives

You *need* food, clothing, and shelter. People have survived horrendous tragedies with very little money or other resources. You *want* a comfortable home, a full pantry, and books or sports or other stuff to entertain you. *Needs* keep you alive, *wants* turn an existence into a lifestyle. The internet has numerous articles that describe Dr. Abraham Maslow and his research, known as "Maslow's Hierarchy of Needs" and the psychology underlying this aspect of the human experience. They make good reading.

Category 1: Needs—What income do I require to survive and maintain health?

This is a category I let each client define. Some are fine as long as they're fed and could live off very little income.

Others might put their travel budget and club memberships as needs. Yours will be different from anyone else's, and every family has to define that number for themselves. I had a conversation recently with a friend who had to sell both his jets because he didn't have liquidity for living expenses. It's always a scary deal to start selling off assets like that.

Category 2: Wants—What makes life fun, fulfilled, worth living?

This list is endless—charitable giving, hunting trips, beach vacations, family reunions, or travel with friends. (I'll mention again that tax-savvy charitable-giving strategies are available that allow us to do good far beyond what most of us might guess we could.)

As we gain wealth, we feel a desire to enjoy the finer things of life. Go for it—you've earned it!

Whatever you want to do, do it within a clear and carefully calculated budget.

Step 2: The Three-Category Investment Framework

Category 1: SPG—30-40 Percent of Your Portfolio

Safe, Predictable, Guaranteed (SPG) investments provide a foundation for economic security. They cover immediate needs with almost zero market risk.

They're always available, don't fluctuate with market crashes, and provide level, predictable payments. Examples include Social Security, pensions, high-yield savings accounts, CDs and Treasury bills, stable-value funds, variable or fixed annuities, and the cash value of life insurance (not available on all policies).

Here's a test question to determine if an investment fits as an SPG: if the market drops by fifty percent, does this still pay me the same amount?

Category 2: Hybrid—40-50 Percent of Your Portfolio

This category produces income now, but that income isn't predictable or guaranteed. It may produce an income stream now, but income from these investments can be subject to decisions by a board or other management.

For example, let's say you own 1,000 shares of QQQ Corp. For the last few years, the stock has paid modest but steady dividends averaging $4.00 per share per year. Unfortunately, a new product line didn't perform as well as expected, and profits are down. The board of directors declared this year's dividend would be $2.00 per share, a drop of fifty percent.

Dividend stocks can be a great investments. Personally, I love mine, but if we have another repeat of the COVID shutdown, in which 200-plus companies that made up the S&P 500 cut off their payments, we'd be up a creek without a paddle if we depended on these alone.

Category 3: Growth—10-20 Percent of Your Portfolio

These produce no income now, but you expect income in the future. You buy into these because they have the prospect of long-term appreciation. They involve higher risk but offer higher potential reward; that's why they're the smallest category in your portfolio. Before you buy in, do your own due diligence (remember the old sage, "A measured paranoia is a vital survival skill") and assure yourself that they have a solid plan to evolve into an income-producing entity. Examples of growth stocks include Apple, Tesla, Amazon, and many others that started as pure speculation—*they were new and untried ideas*. Likewise, raw land for development; art, coins, stamps, and other collectibles; international growth markets; private equity investments; and your primary residence. Cryptocurrencies also fall into this category when you buy for speculative purposes.

The Reality Check

Your primary residence doesn't produce income now; its value lies in meeting a vital need. It also consumes income—taxes, maintenance, mortgages, and more—but the assumption that property values will rise over time is mostly a safe assumption. (Some of that rise can come from renovations or enhancements you add.) Speculation comes into play with rental properties, which do produce income now and should grow in value over time but, again, consume current income. Often, the home is the biggest single asset people own and has the most potential for growth.

However, even there lies some risk. If you bought a family home thirty years ago and have reached empty-nester status, you might have to spend all the "profit" from your old home to buy that retirement condo because of the new location or the overall rise in housing prices. Even then, there are ways to derive income from downsizing.

Precious metals have a way of holding their buying power over time. Back in the early 1960s, a gallon of gas cost about twenty-five cents (*US Bureau of Labor Statistics*, 2023). Before 1965, those quarters in your pocket were made of ninety percent silver, and each one held roughly 0.18 ounces of silver (*US Mint*, 2024). Fast forward to August 2025, with silver trading around $38 an ounce (*Kitco Metals*, 2025), that same pre-1965 quarter would be worth about seven bucks in melt value–enough to cover roughly two gallons of gas in many parts of the country (*US Energy Information Administration* [EIA], 2025). That's the point: while prices move up and down, metals like gold and silver have a long track record of keeping pace with inflation. It's why a lot of investors and financial pros still recommend holding some of the real stuff–the physical coins or bars–rather than just paper or certificate versions (*Forbes*, 2023; *CNBC*, 2024).

The downside of metals is their practicality. Maybe you can go into Costco and buy some physical gold, but you can't turn around and purchase your groceries with it. There are some states that are starting to adopt metals as a form of currency again, but the market has to catch up to it for it to be real. Of course, there's no law to stop you from trading ("bartering") goods and services for coins or anything else, as long as both parties agree. The value of metals is long term, and prices fluctuate but, again, this value is not in price, it's in buying power.

Step 3: Perform a Balance Sheet Audit

Here's an uncomfortable truth: everyone makes emotional decisions with money–regardless of experience or net worth. Men and women alike. The difference isn't whether emotions show up. It's whether you have a system in place to prevent emotions from hijacking your strategy.

Always do your due diligence. Be proactive, not reactive, in all decisions.

The "Big House" Trap

Suppose your business becomes very successful and you decide to sell out and retire or do something new. You also decide your new, wealthier status warrants a bigger house. That bigger mortgage means less portfolio income. (Of course, if you sell the company for $500 million or $1 billion, you won't be worrying about a mortgage, you can pay cash.) For others, those house payments compete with retirement income. Therefore, calculate all the total long-term costs of that mansion before signing on the dotted line. Again, the question is: will you do your due diligence logically or make an emotional decision?

The Dead Asset Trap

Someone came in my office whose entire net worth was tied up in art. Their plan for income? "We'll never sell it." Not a great plan. In most circumstances, assets bought for their beauty, which don't generate income, are dead weight. I told them, "You need to start charging people to walk in your house or something to see it!" (They didn't think that was nearly as funny as I did.)

An Asset Classification Exercise

Part 1–Assign every asset you own into one of three categories:

Income producer, the good stuff you need to protect like your IRA or any business you own.

Income neutral, which is not generating income now but will someday, like your home or growth stocks.

Income consuming, like a fixer-upper house to be rented out. These can be dangerous. Remember the biblical parable of the man who set out to build a house, then found he had insufficient funds to complete it? I don't caution against them; I just recommend caution. You have to see the potential for income that covers all costs and generated profit.

Part 2—Determine your purpose:

Does this asset cover my need for *survival* and *health*?

Defining *survival* is easy—food, clothing, and shelter. Defining *health* is less so. Some of us age well, in full physical health, while others (even some very young) have severe issues that require extensive treatment. Some of us are happy just hanging out at home with the family, a few friends, and the sports channels. Others need more extensive activities, like travel to see the grandchildren.

Does this asset fund my lifestyle of fun and fulfillment?

What makes life worth living? This list, as noted, is endless, but we can set those things aside for a while when finances get tight.

You now have six classes of assets. Any of the three categories can be designed to fund either of the purposes, but each of the six gets treated differently.

For example, a home is a survival asset but can also be an income-consuming asset. On one hand, you own a four-bedroom home for your growing family. On the other hand, you purchase a two-bedroom home you rent out for now and will move into when you downsize as empty-nesters.

Both fulfill, or will fulfill, the same need while one is now income-neutral and the other is now income-producing.

Section 4: Real World Implementation

A client came to me with $2 million in growth stocks, which, as we've mentioned already, is not, in the 21st century, all that much wealth, especially when it produces zero income.

After a serious review of his goals and explaining the reality of his situation to him, he agreed to a complete revamping of his portfolio. We mixed SPG and hybrid investments while keeping a few of the growth stocks. After all the needed due diligence and a lot of careful research, we were able to realize some profit on his investments and create a solid portfolio that will provide him $120,000 in annual income.

He now enjoys real financial independence. Moments like that remind me why we do what we do—it's never just about money. It's about restoring control, confidence, and purpose in someone's life.

Example is for illustrative purposes only. Actual results will vary and may be more or less favorable.

Summary and Conclusion

Common Implementation Mistakes

1. Perfectionism: waiting for the "perfect" investment. Such an animal, if there ever was one, has long since gone extinct.
2. Emotion: chasing hot trends like cryptocurrencies or meme stocks. Remember "Pet Rocks" and "Cabbage Patch Kids"? The inventors and marketers made a lot

of money, but the fire burned hot and burned out fast.

3. Complexity: over-diversification without purpose. Every decision should follow due diligence and contribute to the goals of a long-term plan.
4. Neglect: "set-it and forget-it" is a bad plan. Times and situations change; your approach to your portfolio must change with them.

Success Principles

1. Purpose drives everything—every dollar has a job to do.
2. Systems beat emotions—rules prevent mistakes.
3. Income is our goal—think *cashflow* over *net worth*.
4. Professional coordination—at Pro Capital, the whole team plays a part in making things happen.

Your wealth should aim to:

- Pay you while you sleep
- Survive market crashes
- Grow to beat inflation
- Fund your dreams
- Protect your family and provide a legacy

The Challenge

Take the Market Drop Test and ask yourself:

- What happens to your income if the market drops fifty percent?
- Could you maintain your lifestyle?
- Do you sleep well knowing your plan?

If not–then it may be time to enter **the VAULT**.

Reality Check

Markets are unpredictable:

- Major crashes since 2000 have wiped out thirty to fifty-seven percent of portfolio value.
- Recoveries often take years, not months.
- Even diversification failed in 2022 when both stocks and bonds fell double digits.

Sequence-of-returns risk proves one simple truth: **when** you start using your money can matter more than *how much* you earn. Two investors with the same portfolio can have wildly different outcomes depending on timing.

The Big Picture

The goal isn't to chase the market average–it's to build a system that strives to perform in every season:

- **SPG assets** (safe, predictable, guaranteed) protect you when everything else fails.
- **Hybrid assets** aim to create reliable income while allowing moderate growth.
- **Growth assets** strive to beat inflation and fuel long-term wealth.

Together, these three create a portfolio that works *through* volatility instead of reacting *to* it.

The Last Word—An Unshakable Promise

I know the last few pages hit you with a lot of numbers and charts. It's easy to skim those, but remember, the data isn't the point. It's the *proof* of the concept.

History shows the same truth again and again: **champions don't win games—championship systems do.**

The same is true with wealth. We believe, an orderly, well-built financial system is your best path toward success. You don't have to guess your way to freedom—there's a path, followed by countless families who built security that lasts.

So don't gamble your future. **Design it. Build it. Protect it.**

CHAPTER 8

L – Lifetimes & Legacies

Making Sure That Your Wealth Survives You

Fundamental Ideas:

1. Structure outlives strength.
2. Continuity requires conversion.
3. Liquidity is the love language of the legacy.

Disaster 1: The Prince—and His "Paupers"

Prince Rogers Nelson—the artist known simply as Prince—ranks among the most successful musicians of his generation. Author of an estimated 500 to 1,000 songs and a global superstar performer, he died unexpectedly at age fifty-seven in 2016—without a will. His estate initially reported a taxable value of about $82 million, but the IRS counter-valued it at $163 million (Barclay Damon, 2022).

A lengthy and public court battle followed. Six years later, the estate's administrators and the IRS reached a final valuation of roughly $156 million (Hollywood Reporter, 2022). Under Minnesota intestacy law, his full sister and five half-siblings were recognized as heirs (Henson Efron, 2022). Comerica Bank & Trust, appointed as administrator, received approximately $3 million in fees (Keystone Law, 2022).

When the federal and state estate taxes were paid, nearly two-thirds of Prince's fortune disappeared, leaving his family with only a fraction of what he had built. In the end, close to $100 million—two-thirds of his fortune—slipped through his family's fingers, all because one of the world's greatest performers never built a financial plan.

The Mistakes

- Time: no young person feels their mortality, unless it's been challenged by a near death experience. They delay creating wills, trusts, and other protections.
- Complexity: the greater their wealth, the less likely it is that they know exactly what they own. In addition to the business(es) they have a stake in, they have stocks and bonds; intellectual, personal, and real property; IRAs, and more. Few people, if any, could tell you what they're worth on any given day.
- Privacy Concerns: again, the greater your wealth, the greater your need for privacy to avoid clingers, scammers, and assorted other scoundrels. Most of us want to keep personal matters confidential but the greater your wealth, the greater your need for professional advice. The average (even the well-above-average) person simply isn't trained to manage wealth.
- Misunderstanding the Point: estate planning is not about keeping your money out of the government's hands. That's one of the goals, but financial planning exists to benefit your heirs. That's the goal set by most wealthy people—take care of my loved ones! Estate planning plays three vital roles: it helps grow the wealth you have. It protects what you have and what you can obtain. It prevents disputes among heirs and, especially, with governments.

Disaster 2: James Gandolfini–An Offer He Should've Refused

Actor James Gandolfini, best known for portraying mob boss Tony Soprano in HBO's *The Sopranos*, died suddenly in 2013 at age fifty-one. Although he left a formal will, that single document became his undoing. The will alone governed roughly $70 million in assets, leaving about eighty percent of his estate exposed to taxes–a mistake that resulted in an estimated $30 million estate-tax bill for his heirs (*Forbes*, 2013; *CNBC*, 2019).

His estate included property in both the United States and Italy, as well as luxury cars, fine art, and valuable watches. The will divided his holdings–twenty percent to his daughter, twenty percent to his wife, and the remaining sixty percent to his sisters–while his son received certain personal items and a trust fund. But because there were no irrevocable trusts or other tax-deferral strategies in place, federal estate taxes claimed forty percent of everything above the $5.25 million exemption, and New York's state tax added another three to sixteen percent on top (*New York Times*, 2013). In total, taxes consumed nearly forty-three percent of his estate's value.

Gandolfini's misstep was simple but devastating: he accepted the "offer" that so many do–the illusion that a well-written will equals a complete estate plan. It was, in truth, *an offer he should have refused*. His will provided clarity, but not protection. Without the proper structures–trusts, gifting strategies, or cross-border planning–his fortune became another case study in how even world-class talent can fail the basics of legacy design.

Disaster 3: Elvis Presley–The Queen Saves the Kingdom

When anyone says Elvis, we all know who they mean. The "King of Rock and Roll" reshaped American music forever, and his fame has outlived nearly every peer. But Elvis's legendary generosity and spending habits became just as famous as his voice. He often joked that if he ever ran short, another tour or record would fix it. That mindset kept him beloved–but broke.

When Elvis died in 1977 at just forty-two, his estate was valued by the IRS at roughly $10 million (*Forbes*, 2023). That might sound impressive, but it was only a small portion of his lifetime earnings, estimated between $100 million and $1 billion (*Rolling Stone*, 2017). Even after accounting for taxes and inflation, few modern artists could rival his earning power. Yet, by the time his father Vernon Presley, who served as executor, died two years later, the estate had shrunk to about $1 million due to poor investments, legal fees, and the massive cost of maintaining Graceland (*Smithsonian Magazine*, 2019).

Elvis's will divided his remaining fortune among his father, grandmother, and daughter, Lisa Marie Presley, with Vernon acting as trustee. Though honest and devoted, he lacked the financial sophistication to manage the estate's complexity. Making matters worse, Elvis's longtime manager, Colonel Tom Parker, had siphoned off enormous sums through exploitative contracts–including a fifty-percent commission on a $5.6 million record deal that left Elvis with just $1.35 million and a crushing tax bill (*Los Angeles Times*, 1980).

That might have been the end of the Presley fortune–had it not been for Priscilla Presley, who stepped in after Vernon's death in 1979. She formed Elvis Presley Enterprises, transformed Graceland into a global tourist destination, and invested the proceeds wisely. By Lisa Marie's 25th birthday in 1993, Priscilla had rebuilt the estate's value to nearly $100 million (*Forbes*, 2023; *BBC*, 2017).

The lesson is timeless: it's not enough to have a plan—you must have the *right* plan, guided by the *right* people. Elvis trusted loyalty over literacy, heart over structure. It took the Queen to save the Kingdom.

Three Universal Problems

1. People Put It Off

Most people live like tomorrow is guaranteed. I get it. I've put off stuff too. Most of us are really busy with life and just put it off until something bad happens to us or someone close to us. There's also a lot of people that don't like to think about planning for death, so they just avoid it.

Reality check: Prince was fifty-seven. James Gandolfini was fifty-one. Elvis was forty-two. (And Lisa Marie Presley was only fifty-four.) Death doesn't wait for your estate plan or your schedule. According to the CDC, between ages twenty-six and forty-five, essentially the first half of your working life, roughly 100,000 men and 72,000 women die each year. The leading causes aren't rare diseases or old age, but unintentional injuries, followed closely by cancer and heart disease (*CDC*, 2024).

The truth is that the clock starts ticking the day you start earning. Every person should begin thinking about planning and wealth protection when they start earning money. In fact, many of our clients who employ their children begin teaching them the fundamentals of financial planning before they can even vote.

2. They Think They Can Do It Themselves

Let me repeat some statistics from Chapter 4:

As baby boomers and their parents begin passing their wealth to Generations X, Y, and Z, one report estimates $72 trillion in assets will change hands from the creators to their heirs over the next twenty years.[12].

Trustandwill.com estimates that less than one-third of Americans even have a will, that just eleven percent have a trust, and fifty-five percent have no estate plan at all.[13]

The internet has made so many things so simple that people get this foolish idea that they can do anything.

Some projects are so critical and so complex that they require professionally competent operation.

Speaking of operations, would you ever think to save money by performing surgery on yourself? Ever hear the old saw, "Anyone who represents himself in court has a fool for a lawyer and a jackass for a client"? I could go on, but you get

---

[12] Joseph Coughlin, "The Great Wealth Transfer is Happening but not in the Way You Think," *Forbes.com*. Jersey City, New Jersey: Integrated Whale Media Investments, 26 June 2024 (updated 17 December 2024). https://www.forbes.com/sites/josephcoughlin/2024/06/26/the-great-wealth-transfer-is-happening-but-not-in-the-way-you-think/

[13] Staff, "Who Has an Estate Plan? A Demographic Breakdown," *TrustAndWill.com*. San Diego: Trust&Will, (undated). https://trustandwill.com/learn/2025-report-estate-planning-demographic-breakdown/

the picture. Is your financial strength any less vital than your physical health or less dangerous than your legal protection?

3. The Government Is, Potentially, Your Biggest Heir

As noted earlier, just about every financial rule ever enacted by any government favors that government. The government can't create wealth; it has to take what it needs and wants.

Another myth: "Taxes are theft." No, no, no! Governments have costs and taxes (which include excises, imposts, tariffs, and other such things) fund the government. What you tax, how much you tax, when taxes are due, and a host of other things, might be wise or foolish, constitutional or not, ethical or immoral, but the concept of taxation is a necessity in society, so get used to it. (And, while you're at it, question your political candidates about their feelings on that subject then vote accordingly.)

You might get the idea that taxes are, therefore, inevitable. Well, some are, but not all. The addendum to that busted myth is that every citizen has the right, and many opportunities, to avoid taxes. Again, you need the right plan run by the right people, but you can reduce (in some cases, to $0.00) the taxes you owe on your estate.

If you don't have a solid plan that covers all the bases, Uncle Sam gets rich. Your family gets what's left.

It's just that simple.

The Three Deadly D's

Every wealthy person faces three threats to their legacy. Since this is partly a review, I'm going to put these in Q&A style:

1. Death—The Estate Tax Trap

Question	Answer
How much of my estate is tax-free?	The first $13.61 million of your estate is exempt from federal estate tax. Anything above that amount is taxed at 40 percent.
Who decides what my estate is worth?	Ultimately, the IRS does. Its own appraisers determine fair market value—even if your valuation is lower. Prince and Elvis both learned posthumously that the IRS often thinks your legacy is worth far more than you do.
Can you give me an example?	A $20 million estate has a taxable value of $6.39 million, resulting in roughly a $2.56 million federal estate tax bill.
Do states have their own estate taxes?	Yes. State-level estate taxes apply in Connecticut, Hawaii, Illinois, Maine, Massachusetts, Minnesota, New York, Oregon, Rhode Island, Vermont, Washington, and the District of Columbia.
What about inheritance taxes?	Those are separate—paid by the heirs, not the estate. They're imposed in Iowa, Kentucky, Maryland, Nebraska, New Jersey, and Pennsylvania. If you inherit a 401(k) or IRA, withdrawals are also subject to income tax. Depending on your bracket, that could mean 20–37 percent more in federal tax, plus any state income taxes.

How bad can it get?	Take a $20 million estate in New York: • Federal tax: ≈ $2.56 million • New York State tax: ≈ $2.67 million • Income tax on IRAs (if half the estate is qualified money): ≈ $3 million Total tax bill: ≈ $8.25 million, or 41% of the total estate.
What's the takeaway?	Without proper planning, nearly half of a lifetime's work can disappear into taxes, proof that even great wealth can't outlive poor structure.

Death is just the first punch. But what if you don't die—you just can't act? That's where the second "D" can do even more damage.

2. Disability—Who Makes the Decisions?

Question	Answer
What happens if I can't think clearly anymore?	Your medical team will do everything possible to keep you alive—and bill you for it—while they search for the next of kin to make decisions. If your wishes aren't documented and your decision-makers aren't legally designated, control defaults to whoever the law or hospital policy selects.
Who pays my bills and runs my finances?	Without powers of attorney or trust authorizations, no one can sign checks or access your accounts. Your bills, mortgage, insurance, and investments will still need attention, but banks won't accept a family member's "good intentions" as authorization.

Who runs my business if I'm out?	If you haven't named a successor or created a business continuity plan, your company may stall. As the old saying goes, "Life goes on." The world doesn't wait for your recovery–clients, payroll, and vendors move forward, with or without you.
How long can things operate without me?	If you're properly prepared–with legal documents, funding, and clear succession plans–your world can run indefinitely. They'll notice you're gone, but they'll be able to carry on. That's the point: to protect your family and business, even when you can't.
What's the takeaway?	A strong financial plan isn't just about building wealth–it's about building systems that let life go on when you can't.

If death takes everything suddenly and disability slowly, the third "D" destroys it by choice. It's the one almost no one plans for–until it's too late.

3. Divorce–Protecting Family Assets

Question	Answer
How common is financial ruin after divorce?	Roughly one in seven people who divorce also face bankruptcy soon after. Among women, nearly one in three experience a significant financial setback, and about one in four men face similar challenges. The odds worsen with age.
What happens to business ownership?	In community property states, everything accumulated during the marriage–including businesses–may be subject to equal division. Even outside those states, dividing an enterprise can cause lasting conflict and destroy value.

How can I protect family wealth from divorce or blended-family disputes?	Through prenuptial or postnuptial agreements, trusts, and asset-segregation strategies. Properly titled assets and funded trusts protect both legacy and relationships by clarifying ownership and intent long before emotions run high.
What about second marriages and stepchildren?	These situations require careful documentation. Without it, the courts—not you—decide who inherits what. Proper estate planning avoids infighting and protects biological and blended heirs alike.
Isn't that a little pessimistic?	Not at all. Nobody marries expecting divorce. Marriage is sacred and worth fighting for. But planning for every possibility—including separation—protects the family you built, the business you've grown, and the legacy you want to leave.
What's the takeaway?	If you don't plan it, someone else will. A well-structured plan protects your assets, your family, and your peace of mind—even when life doesn't go according to plan.

Each of these *Three Deadly D's* can dismantle your family's future faster than any market correction or tax law. But with the right structures, you can accommodate for them. That's the power of planning: control, clarity, and continuity, no matter what life throws your way.

The Solution: Advanced Legacy Tools

Notes:

1. Every state has different laws. Work with local attorneys and advisors who know your state's rules and follow them to the letter.

2. These are not all the options, nor are they recommendations for you. These are the more common possibilities for how you can arrange your assets. Each has advantages and disadvantages. Consult your attorney, accountant, and financial planner to choose which options are best suited to your specific situation.

1. The Dynasty Trust

This instrument is designed specifically to keep wealth in your family for the next one hundred years or more.

You put your wealth into a special family trust where your kids get an income, but they don't "own" the money. When they die, they pay no estate tax because they never owned the assets. Your grandkids and great-grandkids can benefit forever. It's best for families with $10 million or more who want generational wealth.

2. The Charitable Remainder Trust (CRT)

This instrument sells assets without paying taxes now and generates lifetime income.

You put appreciated assets (businesses, land, stocks, etc.) in the trust. The trust then sells them with no immediate capital gains tax. You get immediate tax deductions and you get paid an income for your lifetime. When you die, the remainder goes to charities of your choice—hence, the name of the instrument. Best for business owners with highly appreciated assets who also want to help charities.

3. Grantor Retained Annuity Trust (GRAT)

This instrument passes business growth to kids while you keep control.

You transfer part of your business, or other fast-growing assets, to a trust and the trust "pays you back" with fixed payments. Any extra growth goes to your kids tax-free. You continue running the business. Best for fast-growing businesses and younger business owners.

4. Spousal Lifetime Access Trust (SLAT)
This instrument removes money from your estate while the family maintains access.

You put money in trust for your spouse, and the money no longer counts toward your estate tax limit. Your spouse can use money, if needed, and the kids inherit it after the spouse's passing without paying estate tax. Best for married couples worried about estate taxes.

5. Family Limited Partnership (FLP)
This instrument keeps the family in control while reducing estate taxes.

The family business becomes a partnership with the parents maintaining control—they must own fifty-one percent or more. You give the kids partnership shares at a discounted value. This reduces estate and gift taxes significantly. Best for family businesses and real estate investments.

6. Irrevocable Life Insurance Trust (ILIT)
This instrument removes life insurance from your taxable estate.

You set up a trust that owns your life insurance policy and you gift money to trust to pay the premiums. When you die, the payout goes to the trust, not to your estate, and doesn't count toward inheritance tax limits. Your kids get the full amount of your insurance money without any estate taxes.

Best for anyone with large life insurance policies, estate tax bills, or wanting to leave a larger inheritance.

The Asset Titling Crisis

How You Own Things Matters More than What You Own

The shocking truth: over ninety percent of wealthy families have their assets titled incorrectly.

"Titling" simply means who legally owns the assets. You can, literally, own nothing but remain in control of one hundred percent of your wealth and which beneficiary receives them. Your will and trust are just pieces of paper—how assets are titled determines who actually gets them. Common titling mistakes include:

1. When Everything Is in Your Personal Name(s)

Your assets are not protected in a lawsuit. A mistake involving your business could mean losing your home, IRA, and everything else. When you pass away, your estate may be subject to maximum taxes. Even with a will, your estate will likely go through probate court, which costs money and opens your private affairs public, because probate court records are accessible to everyone.

2. Your Beneficiaries List Is Outdated

Is your ex-spouse still listed on your 401(k) or insurance policy or elsewhere? Does your family include kids from previous marriages? Will you include or exclude step-children in any inheritances? Do you have agreements or promises with people not listed in your documents? Who are the beneficiaries listed on your retirement accounts or other things?

You need to look at your will, trust, and other documents regularly to make sure everything is up to date.

3. No Coordination Between Documents Means Court Dates

If your will says one thing and the beneficiary forms for your insurance and other accounts say something else, the court will sort it out—and they don't have your best interest at heart Judges are guided strictly only by the law. You might also have a trust, but assets have to be formally transferred into it. This is a legal change of ownership that has to be documented and, in some cases, registered with government agencies.

The Better Way to Title Assets

Your personal residence should have a joint ownership deed with your spouse or be owned by a trust. Investment accounts should also be held in a trust to simplify ownership transfer on your death and to maintain privacy. Each of your business interests should have a separate legal entity (LLC, S-Corp, corporation, etc.) to protect against a disaster in one damaging the others. Your life insurance needs an Irrevocable Life Insurance Trust (ILIT) to avoid estate taxes. Any retirement accounts need proper beneficiary designations with contingencies in case some beneficiaries pre-decease you.

Business Succession Planning

Who will run your business when you can't? (And, make no mistake, unless you sell the business, the day will come when you can't, either because of death or disability.) You have three options:

1. Keep It in the Family

You can use trusts to transfer ownership gradually. However, if you want the business to continue successfully, it takes more than just good documents. Remember the core risk of generational businesses—that family members might be unqualified or uninterested. Handing your business to someone unprepared is professional suicide. You need to train family members to run the business right. The business needs family employment policies, including treating relatives the same as any other employee. Relatives need to know how every aspect of the business works. They should understand how every aspect of the business works—at least in general terms—including your role, along with bookkeeping, marketing, and other key functions. Finally, relatives must be promoted on merit, not genealogy.

2. Sell to Key Employees

Selling to employees removes several risks in family transfers: they must be qualified, or they wouldn't be key employees. They must want the business to succeed, or they'd go work somewhere else. You can set up a management buyout over time. The primary risk is employees who don't have money to make the purchase when the owner is ready to sell. Long-term planning, using seller financing or any of a number of other options, can ease that problem. Finally, consider staying involved as advisor for a time; help smooth the transition by informing the major clients and vendors of the process.

3. Sell to Outsiders

If you have a solid business, there might be many private equity firms or competitors who'd purchase your business. This has a major advantage: you get cash from the equity firm immediately or stock in the competitor firm that could produce long-term income. There's also a major disadvantage in that you lose control. Once an equity firm takes over, you're history. In a competitor merger, you might have a seat on the board, but you can be outvoted on any matter. There's also the question of business culture and how it will change. The new owners may have very different views on how "your" business should be run. How will that affect your employees, clients, vendors, or your personal reputation?

Key Questions to Ask before You Decide:
- Who has the *skills* to run the business?
- Who actually *wants* to run it?
- How do you treat family versus employees fairly?
- How do you want yourself and your business to be remembered?

Pro Tip

Wealthy people can afford the best advisors in the world, and many of them still get it wrong.

You can learn from others' mistakes and start planning today by making the right choices.

Ninety percent of wealthy families lose their wealth by the third generation because they didn't plan the transfer properly.

Your great-grandchildren will either thank you or never know your name.

You can't take it with you. You will leave a legacy. Don't leave it to the government.

CHAPTER 9

T – Taxes & Time

Leveraging More of What You Make and Working Less Than You Think

Fundamental Ideas:

1. Tax planning is not optional—"failing to plan is planning to fail."
2. It's not at all about what you make; it's all about what you keep.

Taxes are one of the biggest things we have people (and myself) cussing about. It's needed for our government to function, but to think about all the ways we're taxed just eats away at your soul when you work so hard to create it. Even more so when the government wastes so much!

That being said, tax planning is a necessary function of money that needs to be incorporated. As much as I love my CPAs and accountants, I still jump on them to help find new ways to minimize our tax bill this year and going forward. Sometimes it's not always clear which choice to make, but sometimes it is. That's why we use various tools to help us make decisions.

Let's see if we can expand a bit on some ideas, stories, and categories that are important to consider:

Part 1: Tax Management

Facts That Will Change How You View Taxes

1. Taxes are not another bill; they are your single largest lifetime expense.
High earners, thirty to fifty percent of your lifetime income will go to federal, state, sales, and other taxes. Compare that to:

- Housing: approx. twenty to twenty-five percent of lifetime income.
- Healthcare: approx. ten to fifteen percent of lifetime income.
- Raising children: approx. seven to twelve percent of lifetime income.

Question: if you're willing to shop around for a mortgage rate to save $200 to $300 per month, why wouldn't you seek to enhance the expense that costs you hundreds of thousands or millions over your lifetime?

2. Like interest, taxes compound—disastrously.
Example: Growth of a $1 million investment over thirty years at eight percent return:

- In a tax-free account (like a Roth IRA) will grow to approx. $10 million.
- In a taxable account (paying twenty percent of your gross) will grow to approx. $6 million.

The difference, $4 million, was lost to the bureaucracy. Both accounts earn interest, but you only earn interest on what you keep. From what the government takes, you get nothing (but heartburn).

Note: This is a hypothetical example that is demonstrating a mathematical principal. It does not illustrate any investment products and does not show past or future performance of any specific investment.

3. Rules for business owners are different than rules for paycheck employees.

- Choosing the right entity (LLC vs S-Corp) can save 15.3 percent on self-employment taxes.
- Advanced retirement plans let owners defer $100,000+ per year in taxes.

Most business owners don't know these (and other) rules exist. An old sage once said, "I didn't know enough to know that I didn't know enough." All of us (except those who are insanely egotistical) know that we don't know everything. The wise among us look for and hire people who know more than we do.

4. Tax rate changes—timing matters.

The difference between death and taxes is death doesn't get worse every time Congress meets.

–Will Rogers

- The top marginal rate for the US federal income tax has been as high as ninety-four percent—that should scare you!

When the modern federal income tax was introduced through the *Revenue Act of 1913*, the lowest bracket began at just one percent, while the top rate was seven percent on income over $500,000—about $11 million in today's dollars (*Revenue Act of 1913*, US Department of the Treasury).

During World War I, Congress quickly raised the top bracket to sixty-seven percent to fund the war effort (*Tax Policy Center*, 2023). By World War II, the top marginal rate had soared to ninety-four percent on income over $200,000, roughly $2.5 million today.[14] In the 1980s, sweeping tax reform dropped the top rate from around seventy percent to twenty-eight percent, with lawmakers promising it would never climb that high again—a promise that lasted barely three years (*Tax Foundation*, 2023). By the 1990s, the top rate had fallen below forty percent, where it has remained ever since. Today's thirty-seven percent top marginal rate is, historically speaking, one of the lowest levels the United States has seen in more than a century (*Concord Coalition*, 2023).

- With record federal debt, most experts project higher future taxes.

Sooner or later, spending must be cut or taxes increased to service the $37 trillion (as of September 2025) federal debt. No experts are betting that Congress will cut spending.

If you don't plan now, with a Roth conversion, trusts, gifting, or other strategies, you risk paying a far larger bill later.

5. Legacy without planning is a tax disaster.
To repeat:

- Federal and state governments tax success—yours!

I repeat the myth: "Taxes are theft." No, taxation is necessary; they fund government services like roads, law enforcement,

---

[14] teachinghistory.org. "Tax Rates of the Mid-20th Century," 2022. https://teachinghistory.org/history-content/ask-a-historian/24489.

and Social Security. We should be complaining about unethical taxes, like estate taxes, which penalize success. Will that ever change? That depends on who you send to Congress or your state legislature.

- Up to $84 trillion is being transferred to younger generations. That is, potentially, billions of dollars in federal and state revenue and they want it bad!

The IRS appraised the estates of Prince and Elvis, possibly overvaluing them. Remember that old joke, "Hi, I'm from the government. I'm here to help"? You don't want to end up the punchline of that joke!

- Tax planning determines whether heirs receive it or the IRS does.

The rule book for taxation (the IRS Code) includes numerous ways to shelter your wealth from taxes. All perfectly legal, most widely unknown. Failure to take advantage of these legal loopholes is a failure to protect your estate and heirs from the federal government.

The Problem

The $2.8 Million Mistake That Didn't Have to Happen

This client came to us after the fact. This was a land deal, but similar things could happen with other types of assets. There are different tax classes and regulations for different types of assets, but this one serves as a good example of the general principle.

Several years ago, a gentleman we'll call "Donovan" bought a piece of land in Alabama for just over $1 million. It was farmland, and it brought him a small but steady income—a very common situation. Until, that is, several major companies—an internet retailer, a car manufacturer, a sports equipment manufacturer, and a supplier for the car company—built facilities directly around this farmland. Someone decided to expand and offered Don $10.8 million for the dirt. (I would have responded, "$15 million and it's yours!" but that's just me.)

So, he bought for $1 million and accepted the $10.8 million. Who wouldn't? This was amazing, exactly what you want from an investment, right?

Now, sometimes, in their excitement, people's common sense sometimes goes out the window. In this case, Don went to a bunch of his rich buddies. Conventional wisdom (which, generally, isn't very wise) says he did the right thing by going to successful people he knew and trusted for advice. Sadly, they were successful in other areas, not financial planning. Don asked, "What would you do?"

Essentially, they just shrugged their shoulders and said, "You should definitely sell it, then pony up the government's cut." These successful people, by the way, included his CPA and his attorney. They all seemed to have a very "ho-hum" mindset, agreeing that Don should just go and pay taxes, which is what largely ended up happening. (They also agreed to a "government's cut," as if the government were a partner in the property's ownership.)

So, the $1 million investment became a $10.8 million sale, yielding a $9.8 million profit. Well done all around, right?

Here's the thing: once you complete the transaction, take the cash, and put it in your bank account, the tax situation is set. You can't reverse that transaction. He was in the top tax bracket at that point. So, first, we have a twenty percent federal capital gains rate, plus the 3.8 percent Medicare surcharge on top of that. Then, Alabama imposed a five percent state tax against the total. The final bill is 28.3 percent of the profit–$2,773,400 altogether.

His profit was now reduced to $7,026,600. That's still at tidy sum on its own, but it's not $9.8 million. He lost well over one quarter of his profit to the government and probably cussed all the way to the bank.

Real Tax Problems

1. The "pay and pray" mentality. Most wealthy people view taxes as an inevitability and simply pray they paid enough to avoid being audited. Some taxes are unavoidable, but you wouldn't accept the first price on a house or car, so why accept the first tax bill?

2. Most CPAs are tax filers, not tax planners. Most CPAs file your tax return in April or request an extension. They focus only on this year's tax bill. They don't look backward for missed opportunities, and they don't look forward by planning long-term strategies.

You need year-round tax planning, multi-year tax strategies, investment tax management, and business structure planning.

3. Missing the time value of tax savings. In our example story, the seller could have used the IRS's own regulations to defer those taxes, putting that money to work for him and his family.

The Solution: Understanding the Three Tax Worlds

The key to tax management is what, where, and how you invest.

The Good News

In Donovan's case, we were able to catch a portion of it. We were able to defer a portion of that capital gains tax using a "1031 exchange." (The "1031" refers to the section of the IRS Code that oversees these transactions.) It allows an owner to sell real estate, gas, or oil assets and defer the taxes on the profits by reinvesting them into other real estate, gas, or oil assets. The seller can put those profits into one new asset or spread the money over several investments.

As you know, if you buy a house and it appreciates in value, you'll pay capital gains on the appreciation when you sell it, unless you use that money to purchase another house. (If you use only parts of the proceeds, you pay capital gains on the unused portion.) A 1031 exchange works the same way.

We took $3 million of Donovan's profit and invested it in other similar assets, saving him just under $1 million in taxes. We used a section of the tax code that specifically allows us to do this. I think it's one of the best pieces of our tax code, along with similar sections that deal with other types of investments. Had we been involved from the get-go, we could have saved him even more.

There are other options: a 721 exchange does something similar using a real estate investment trust (UPREIT), a 1035 exchange deals with insurance contracts, and so on. All these give you a tax break if you reinvest your money because that benefits the whole economy, instead of putting in in your checking account, which benefits you alone. No, the IRS hasn't gone soft in its old age; the government expects those new investments to be profitable for you and they hope that the future profits will ultimately generate more taxes for them to waste.

Had we met the client before he completed the transaction, we could've placed all those profits into growth and income opportunities, pulling in three to four percent (conservatively) for decades to come. At four percent, $10.8 million would return $432,000 in gross annual income that Donovan was not living off before the sale.

Imagine retiring on $36,000 per month for the rest of your life!

Every "professional" he spoke to said the same thing, with a shrug, "Well, you might as well pay the taxes, they aren't going away."

We showed him that he didn't have to pay those taxes; we could convert that cash into income-producing assets generating substantial annual income, even assuming he just got a reasonable return. That wealth, by the way, could also have been structured so that Don could pass his wealth on to the next generation tax-free.

There's far more to taxes than filing a return. Some taxes cannot be avoided, you just pay them and move on. But we have our ways to minimize those taxes.

Explore all your options with a professional before making any decision.

The Three Tax Buckets

Any investments or strategies referenced herein do not consider the investment objectives, financial situation, or needs of any specific person. Product suitability must be independently determined for each individual investor.

1. The Tax-Deferred Bucket gives you a tax deduction now. You place pre-tax dollars in traditional IRAs and 401(k)s, SEP-IRAs and Solo 401(k)s, defined benefit plans, traditional annuities, and some business structures. You pay taxes on the money you withdraw after you retire.

Some investments to consider for this bucket are bonds (since interest is taxed as ordinary income anyway), REITs (which typically have high dividend yields), high-turnover mutual funds, and other assets that generate ordinary income.

This makes sense when you're in a high tax bracket—a business owner or paycheck employee. You're making real money now and you're stuck in a high-tax bracket, but you expect to be in lower bracket after retiring. You need tax deductions now.

For example: a business owner earning $500,000 puts $100,000 into a defined benefit plan. He saves $37,000 in taxes this year, as he's in the thirty-seven percent bracket. That money grows tax-deferred until retirement. (Hopefully, tax rates have gone down along with your income needs at that point.)

2. The Tax-Free Bucket means you never pay taxes on the return from this money. You put after-tax money (receiving no deduction now) into a Roth IRA or Roth 401(k), cash value life insurance, a health savings account (HSA—triple tax exempt), a 529 education plan, or certain municipal bonds.

Investments to consider for this bucket might include the highest-growth-potential stocks, small-cap and international growth, assets expected to multiply in value, and volatile investments with big upsides.

This makes the most sense when you're young and have a long-term time horizon. You expect higher tax rates in the future, and you want tax-free income in retirement and in estate planning for your heirs.

Example: a thirty-five-year-old has $10,000 in a Roth IRA investing in aggressive growth stocks. It grows to $500,000 by retirement, and he pays zero taxes on the $490,000 gain.

A Roth IRA distribution is qualified if you've had the account for at least five years and/or the distribution is made after you've reached age 59 ½, due to total and permanent disability, upon your death, or for first-time homebuyer expenses. Distributions made prior to age 59 ½ may be subject to a federal income tax penalty.

3. The Taxable Bucket means you pay taxes as you go—on interest, dividends, and gains each year when you invest in a regular brokerage account, individual stocks and bonds, mutual funds, exchange-traded funds (ETFs), real estate investments, or certain business investments.

Investments for this bucket might include tax-efficient index funds, individual growth stocks that you hold more than one year, and municipal bonds for high earners, and other assets you might need before retirement.

This makes sense when you need a lot of flexibility to access your money, want to harvest tax losses, don't qualify for retirement accounts, or are saving for goals you plan to hit before retirement. You'll need to hold these investments for more than one year to qualify for capital gains rates, offset gains by harvesting losses, donate appreciated stocks to charity, and use tax-efficient fund strategies.

High-Level Tax Planning for Your Business

Entity Structure Optimization

Entity Type	Self-Employment Tax	Income Tax	Best For
Sole Proprietorship	15.3% on all income	Regular rates	Very small businesses
LLC	15.3% on all income	Regular rates	Simple structure, asset protection
S-Corp Election	Only on salary portion	Regular rates	$60,000+ profit, want tax savings
C-Corp	None	21% corporate + personal	Large businesses that want to retain earnings

For example, if you elect S-Corp status and have a business profit of $200,000, you can pay yourself an $80,000 salary that's subject to payroll, Medicare, and other taxes, just like a paycheck employee. You can then take $120,000 as profit distribution—you pay no payroll tax on that portion, while the business pays the corporate taxes. Your savings are $120,000 × 15.3% = $18,360 per year.

Business Retirement Plan Strategies

A 401(k) for business owners means an employee contribution of up to $23,000 (in 2024), with an employer contribution up to twenty-five percent of compensation. The total possible contribution is $69,000 per year ($76,500 if you're over age fifty).

A defined benefit plan for high earners means you can contribute $100,000 to $300,000-plus annually, based on age and income. A fifty-year-old earning $500,000 can contribute over $200,000.

A cash balance plan is a hybrid approach—it combines 401(k) and pension benefits with age-weighted contributions favoring older owners, allowing you to contribute $200,000 or more annually for high earners.

Business Tax Deduction Strategies

The Augusta Rule (IRS Code Section 280A) allows you to rent your home to your business up to fourteen days per year. The business deducts rent from its profits and you get tax-free income. At $1,500 per day for fourteen days, that means $21,000 tax-free. (You will be expected to demonstrate that the home was, in fact, used primarily for business purposes during that period.)

Hiring family members is perfectly legal; you just need to put your spouse and children on the payroll in some legitimate capacity. For example, a wedding/family photographer has a baby and takes the usual beautiful baby-bragging photos. He or she can pay that child a sitting fee (just like any professional model), up to whatever the standard deduction is for that year—that's $13,850 tax-free in 2024. The business gets a deduction, the family saves on taxes, and those fees can fund Roth IRAs for children or an IRS Code Section 529 fund for education. (Note: 529 plans are federally-authorized but state run, and each state has its own rules, including limitations.)

Summary of Investment Tax Management

Discuss these possibilities with your financial planner. Plan your asset location strategy carefully, putting the right investments in the right accounts:

Investment Type	Best Account	Reason
Growth Stocks	Roth IRA or Taxable	Treated like capital gains
Bonds	Tax-deferred	Avoids ordinary income tax
REITs	Tax-deferred	Offer high dividend yields
International Stocks	Tax-deferred	Foreign tax credit benefits
Municipal Bonds	Taxable	Already tax-free
Small Cap Growth	Roth IRA	Highest growth potential

Capital Gains Management

Short-Term versus Long-Term:

Short-term means under one year and are taxed as ordinary income (up to thirty-seven percent). Long-term means over one year and is taxed at referential rates (zero percent, fifteen percent, or twenty percent). Hold on to growth investments over one year when possible.

Tax Loss Harvesting:
You can sell losing investments to offset gains or use losses to reduce ordinary income (up to $3,000 per year) and carry forward unused losses indefinitely. Avoid the "wash sale" rules, that is, don't buy same investment within thirty days of selling one.

Real Estate Tax Advantages

Residential rental properties depreciate over 27.5 years, while commercial properties depreciate over thirty-nine years. You can defer all capital gains taxes using 1031-type exchanges. When you sell investment assets, buy others. You can repeat this process indefinitely, but there are strict timelines and rules you must follow.

Find local "economically-distressed areas" that have been designated "opportunity zones." Invest capital in those areas, and you can defer taxes. Potentially, if you hold assets ten-plus years, your growth can be tax-free.

Income Tax Management Strategies for High-Income Business Owners

Income smoothing accelerates deductions in high-income years by allowing you to defer income under certain circumstances. You can also use retirement plans to manage brackets. This can be especially valuable at bonus time around the end of the year.

Charitable giving can improve tax savings by donating appreciated stock instead of cash. You'll avoid capital gains tax on the appreciation and get full fair-market value as a deduction. For example, if you bought stock for $10,000 and it has grown to be worth $50,000, give that stock to a 501(c)3 and save $8,000 or more in capital gains tax.

Your state of residence is another tax planning consideration for retirees. Some states have no income tax—Texas, Florida, Nevada, among them. Timing your move from state to state might also affect taxation. If you have multi-state business operations, you have multi-state tax considerations.

Investment Income Management

Your dividend strategy should focus on qualified dividends that are taxed at capital gains rates over non-qualified dividends that are taxed as ordinary income. Consider dividend timing around the end of every year. Will that boost you into a higher bracket?

Interest income must be managed. Municipal bonds are better for high earners; I-bonds or TIPS can be valuable for inflation protection, and treasury securities are only subject to federal taxation.

Part 2: Time Leverage

The Time Leverage Revelation

Question: I can build my own website, I can do my own marketing, I can handle my own bookkeeping—should I?

Answer: No! And here's why: every hour you spend doing $50 tasks costs you $4,950 in opportunity.

The $5,000/Hour versus $50/Hour Dilemma

The question every entrepreneur must answer: do you want to spend your time on a $50-per-hour (or less) task or a $5,000-per-hour task?

Those $50-per-hour (or less) tasks include building your website, doing your bookkeeping, managing your calendar, writing your marketing copy, and handling customer service issues.

Those $5,000-per-hour tasks include strategic business planning, fostering client relationships, new product development, creating key partnership deals, and investment decision-making.

Simple math changes everything: spending ten hours building a website yourself costs you $500. Instead, hire a higher-quality professional for $100 per hour who will produce a better product faster than you could yourself. Meanwhile, you have freed up ten hours for $5,000-per-hour work. Spend $1,000 or earn $50,000? That's a $49,000 gain—and the beginning of true time leverage.

The Fresh Eyes Advantage

Why does hiring an expert beat DIY? They see what you can't, bringing a fresh perspective to your problems. Their experience from working with similar businesses brings industry best practices you may not know. They hear and see what you might miss, ask questions you never thought to ask, offer solutions you never knew existed, and issue warnings about mistakes you might make. They deliver faster results, with years of experience compressed into weeks of action. They've already made the learning-curve mistakes, so you don't have to, and they know their professional tools and processes.

The Learning Curve Reality

You might have to experiment with several professionals to find the right fit. That's okay—that's part of the process. The alternative is spending months or years learning something yourself and making expensive mistakes along the way. Try the framework below that helped me turn my business into something far more profitable in both money and time, so I could spend more with my family, travel, and execute higher-value tasks that excited me and ultimately paid more.

The Professional Leverage Framework

Hire experts who can do it faster and better.

<table>
<tr><td>Level 1: Virtual Assistants ($5–$20/hour)
Calendar management, email management, basic research, data entry.</td></tr>
<tr><td>Level 2: Skilled Specialists ($25–$75/hour)
Bookkeeping, marketing assistance, customer service, administrative support, writing coach.</td></tr>
<tr><td>Level 3: Professional Experts ($100–$500/hour)
CPA/tax planning, legal advice, marketing strategist, business coach.</td></tr>
<tr><td>Level 4: Strategic Partners ($500–$2,000/hour or more)
Investment banker, wealth manager, board advisors, strategic consultants.</td></tr>
</table>

Success comes from matching the right expertise to the right task. You don't need to do everything, you need to lead the people who do.

The Bottom Line

The tax code rewards leverage—financial and human. When you delegate, you free yourself to operate where your value is highest. Your time is your greatest asset; spend it like an investor, not a laborer.

When people hire *you*, whether it's for your business, your advice, or your leadership, they're not paying for your hands–they're paying for your *head*. They're paying for the decisions only you can make, the vision only you can see, and the leadership only you can deliver.

That's why I tell people: the most successful entrepreneurs I know don't just hire people to *do* work. They hire people to *get their time back*. That's the real trade, exchanging low-value tasks for high-value time. When you build that system around you, your productivity multiplies, your stress drops, and your earning power explodes.

When people hire my firm, they're doing the same thing. They're hiring professionals who have answers, can fix issues, and get access to their circles. They can tell you if an idea can work or not. They can bring you back to reality or break something loose in your life that you never even heard of.

We handle the planning, strategy, and complexity, freeing them to focus on the things that build their business, strengthen their family, and create legacy. That's time leverage. It's not just a scheduling tool–it's a wealth strategy. Some call it human capital, because every minute you waste $50-per-hour work is time stolen from the $5,000-per-hour life you're trying to build.

Part III
The Implementation
From Knowledge to Action

CHAPTER 10

THE VAULT ASSESSMENT

Fundamental Ideas:

1. Don't get so busy building the castle that you forget to dig the moat.
2. Protect what you have before you work to get more.
3. No system has any value if it isn't implemented consistently.

Where You Are and Where You Need to Go

Most financial advisors or money managers start and end with the money. Although we do important things like financial planning and asset management, if that's all we focused on and an event came along and wiped out all your money, there's no performance or plan in the world that would mean anything at that point. It just becomes a number—and frankly, that much more to lose.

The "We're Fine" Illusion

I'll never forget this couple, because they reminded me that pride is the enemy of preparation. The wife was kind, respectful, and engaged. She took notes the entire time. But the husband walked in like he was auditioning for an alpha-male contest. The second he shook my hand, I knew exactly what was coming—the overcompensating power grip, the lean-in, the test. I remember thinking, *"Dude, I'm bigger than you, and I used to push NFL linemen around for a living."* I've experienced it a lot.

We sat down, and his first words were, "Just so you know, we're fine."

I smiled. "Okay. Then why are you here?"

He smirked. "Well, for my kids… they might need some help."

And the dance began. As I asked questions, he dodged them, giving half-answers and changing the subject. At one point, he said, "So, do you still get a pension from football?"

"Why are you asking me about that?" I said. "We're not talking about me."

Then he put his hand in my face.

I looked him dead in the eye. "Don't do that." Disrespect I can handle. But what came next, I couldn't let slide. When I turned to his wife with a question, she started to answer, and he cut her off, waving his hand in front of her. "No, no, no."

That was it. "No," I told him. "Not in my office. Don't disrespect your wife in my office." She sat up straighter. It was like she'd been waiting for someone to stand up to him.

So I leaned in. The meeting lasted about an hour. I pressed him on everything. Every time he said, "We're fine," I asked, "Show me how. What's your plan for this? What's your plan for that? What's your protection if you get sued?"

He had no answers. Just ego.

Finally, he said, "I know the probabilities. I'll be fine."

"Probability?" I asked. "You know the numbers behind that?"

He didn't.

So I told him: "There's over a thirty percent chance you'll get sued in your lifetime. At any given time, about one in eight Americans are being sued. And in our neighborhoods, where average incomes are over $200,000, those odds get worse. Still fine?"

He froze.

At the end, I said thank you to the wife for her respect and attention, but I wasn't interested in working with her husband. I don't think he had any real intent anyway. Those people just want free information and a free lunch. He was one of the most patronizing people I've ever experienced.

That meeting became a lesson I'll never forget. The "we're fine" mindset is pride dressed up as peace. It's the most dangerous phrase in wealth planning because it shuts down curiosity and humility—two things every successful person needs to keep growing.

The truth is, you need to be careful with the "we're fine" mindset. You honestly could be just fine, but a lot of times it presents itself as fake confidence. Sometimes it's pride, and sometimes it's fear. Whatever the emotion or posture, if left unchecked, can cost more than any lawsuit, tax, or market crash ever could.

The VAULT Assessment

I've sat with a great number of successful entrepreneurs whom you'd think would have everything buttoned up. They had accountants, attorneys, and investment advisors. Their businesses were thriving. Their portfolios were growing. By all appearances, they were financially successful.

Yet within our first conversation, using the VAULT Assessment, we aim to uncover vulnerabilities that could destroy decades of wealth building in a matter of months—or even weeks.

This isn't about fear-mongering. It's about waking you out of your slumber. The same drive and focus that makes entrepreneurs successful often creates blind spots in their wealth protection.

The Financial Director Approach

At Pro Capital, we don't function as traditional investment advisors. We serve as the financial directors of our clients' lives in the same way a business has a controller or chief financial officer (CFO).

As you probably know, the US government has numerous agencies that contribute to creating federal fiscal policy: the Federal Reserve Board, the Council of Economic Advisors, the Office of Management and Budget—even Congress gets to put two cents in. It's the Secretary of the Treasury (SecTreas) that brings it all together. As the federal government's CFO, the SecTreas presents to the President the sum total of "This we know" and "This we think we know," therefore, "This is our best guess about what will happen in the economy." The President then creates his economic initiatives based, in large measure, on those recommendations.

You need a CFO to coordinate the business that is your family's finances.

What I've seen in our industry, and what I experienced personally before I got into it, tells me it doesn't work as smoothly or as well as it should. Most money managers start and end with the money; they don't go anywhere else. Their goal is getting the money–your money–under their management. These assets under management (AUM) are the basis for their compensation. Since they don't profit by worrying about taxes, wills, business organization, or other things, they rarely think about those facets of your wealth.

As a result, your growing wealth means a growing team of advisors, including family lawyers, tax lawyers, accountants, portfolio managers, and so on, plus a seemingly endless stream of data that you're supposed to take in, chew, digest, and get nourishment from, so to speak.

No wonder so many people have heartburn.

You wouldn't run a commercial business with a marketing team, operations team, and finance team that never communicate with each other. Yet most wealthy families do exactly that with their financial planning. The CPA isn't talking to the investment advisor. The estate planning attorney isn't coordinating with the insurance agent. Each is working in a silo. The result? Gaps, overlaps, missed opportunities, and dangerous vulnerabilities.

In one case, we caught a mistake worth $1.5 million. It wasn't a mistake on the part of the tax lawyer or the accountant; they actually did their jobs correctly. But they did only their individual jobs–the mistake was lack of coordination.

In the Bible, we're warned that doing good in public is its own reward. If we want God to recognize it, we should do it for charity's sake, not for man's praise. Jesus went so far as to say, "Let not thy left hand know what thy right hand doeth" (Matthew 6:3).

Great advice if you're helping neighbors fix their fence; disastrous financial advice.

At Pro Capital, we want to be your SecTreas, the hub of the wheel with all your other advisors as the spokes. Together, the wheel rolls smoothly. That's why our assessment process follows a methodology opposite to what most advisors do. Instead of starting with your investments, we start by identifying what could destroy them.

The VAULT Assessment Framework

Before we help you grow your wealth, we need to ensure you can protect what you already have.

The first five chapters have explained, in detail, how we do that. A brief review:

Phase 1: The Vision & Values Discovery (V)

We start with your *purpose*, by asking the critical questions: what does wealth mean to your family? What are you trying to accomplish over the next three generations? What keeps you awake at night about your financial future? If something happened to you tomorrow, what would happen to your family's wealth?

This isn't just a getting-acquainted conversation. These questions reveal the gaps between your current financial structure and your actual goals. Remember, ninety percent of wealthy families lose their fortune by the third generation and less than half of that is related to poor investment performance, the rest results from family dysfunction, lack of communication, and misaligned values.

The Vision & Values conversation identifies potential "train wrecks" that could derail your ability to have the retirement and legacy you want, while also looking for opportunities–during your lifetime or at death–to take care of the people you care about.

Phase 2: The Asset Protection & Acceleration Review (A)

This is where we shift from vision to vulnerability: if you were sued tomorrow, what assets could be taken? How are your business and personal assets structured? Could a single incident wipe out decades of wealth building? Are your assets positioned for both protection *and* growth?

Most people think they have to choose between protection and performance. Most don't realize that the legal structures which protect your assets can also accelerate their growth.

Part of this review is what we call the "Train Wreck Assess-ment," in which we systematically evaluate the most com-mon destroyers of wealth: lawsuit vulnerability; divorce exposure–yours or your children's; business liability risks; estate tax exposure; inadequate insurance coverage; and poor asset titling.

Phase 3: The Unshakable Systems Analysis (U)

Can your wealth survive without your constant attention? Do your income streams continue to flow if you can't work? Are your investments systematized, or are they dependent on market timing? Do you have written investment policies and procedures? Could your spouse or children understand and manage your wealth structure?

The 80/20 Wealth Rule: most successful people are great at making money but terrible at systematizing it. They're constantly managing instead of building systems that manage themselves. They never understand that eighty percent of their success will come from twenty percent of their effort and, therefore, don't allocate their time and effort as effectively as they could.

Phase 4: The Legacy & Lifetimes Review (L)

Notice the plural: *lifetimes*. What does your estate plan actually say? (Most people don't know.) How will your wealth be distributed to your children? Are you accidentally creating entitled heirs or empowered persons? Does your current plan account for inflation and growth over the next twenty to thirty years?

Here's a question that always gets attention: should one of you pass away, do your current estate planning documents require the survivor to sign a valid prenuptial agreement with a future spouse before remarriage? The answer is almost always "no" because most people have never seen (or even heard) of this provision. Likewise, they think a prenup is to protect *their* marriage, not to protect *their children* in a widow's or widower's subsequent marriage.

Here's the reality: if you die first, your spouse has access to all your money for their lifestyle. If they get remarried and don't sign a prenup, there's a chance they could end up leaving your half of the money to that new spouse and, eventually, to that person's children—not to yours!

Phase 5: The Tax Management & Time Leverage Evaluation (T)

Finally, we evaluate whether you're actually keeping what you earn. Are you paying more in taxes than you legally should? Do you just have a CPA doing compliance, or are you identifying real strategies to reduce taxes? Are you using every business-owner advantage available to you? And just as important, is your **time** being deployed where it produces the highest return?

The "Pause" Moment

In our early meetings, when we find an issue, we'll often stop and pause to allow the moment to sink in. When a client explains their current setup, there are times we intentionally *don't* jump in to fix it. Instead, we pause. We let the statement sit. Sometimes we'll say something simple like, "Okay. That's helpful." Or, "I see that a lot." Or, "Interesting."

And then we move on.

This isn't being evasive. It's being disciplined. We don't solve complex problems in introductory meetings—and we don't give away decades of experience for free. The VAULT Assessment exists for a reason: to surface blind spots and pressure-test assumptions people *thought* were solid. Here are a few examples of what triggers that pause:

- **"All of our accounts are just titled jointly."** → *Pause.*
- **"The kids get everything outright if something happens to us."** → *Pause.*
- **"We don't really carry much life insurance."** → *Pause.*
- **"My business partner and I just have a handshake agreement."** → *Long pause.*

We don't need to lecture in that moment. The silence does the work. By the end of the assessment, most prospects feel something very specific: **clarity mixed with urgency**. They realize the plan they believed was "pretty good" is actually fragmented, exposed, and overly dependent on luck. They also realize something else—we *see* the problems, and we're choosing not to solve them yet. That's intentional. Because real solutions require structure, strategy, and execution. And that only happens once we're officially engaged. The goal isn't to overwhelm—it's to wake people up. And Phase 5 is where most high-income earners realize the truth: making good money is not the same thing as keeping it—or controlling where it goes.

Coordination, Not Abdication

We work with numerous clients whose asset portfolios range widely. Whether your estate is $1 million or $100 million, there's always an incident that could wipe you out completely in a day. If that day comes, the $1 million or $100 million is just a number—and that number becomes $0.00!

Our assessment differs from other firms—we're not trying to replace your other advisors; we're trying to coordinate them into a cohesive team with synergy.

One Belgian draft horse can pull about 800 pounds; two, working together, can pull close to 2,400 pounds. That is synergy!

We assume you already have relationships with professionals. We're here to quarterback a successful team strategy by making sure everyone is working at their best toward the same goals.

Here's our one requirement: if we bring you an investment or planning idea that you choose to implement, we expect you to implement it through Pro Capital. We're happy to work with your other advisors, but we're not interested in training them to do what we do. Our ideas are valuable, and we need to be compensated for them—just as you are in your business.

If your professionals don't have the knowledge or experience to see the problem, they probably don't have the knowledge or experience to fix it!

By the way, we advise—we won't strap you into a stroller and roll you down the road. If you've built a portfolio that meets our level of knowledge, you're pretty good at what you do—and at life in general. You don't need us to hold your hand.

I mention this because a recent client came to us from "another" financial advisor service—a name you'd probably recognize if I mentioned it. The client was an NFL player whose father was co-owner in a business being sold to a group of overseas investors for $220 million. They promised to get on the phone every week and do this and that. Dad hired this big advisor firm only to find that the firm over-promised and under-delivered.

Officially, we have a semi-annual, structured review. Lately, however, we've become more flexible, giving the clients a choice in how often we meet because different clients have different needs and schedules.

Sometimes, of course, I get a laugh out of it. I have guys that are saying, "Hey, give me a shout on the third Friday of every month." So I do—but he's always golfing that day and never picks up his phone. We also see the opposite attitude: clients who say, "Don't call me, I'll call you when I need you."

I spoke to a potential client recently who thought that quarterly meetings were the norm. He said that's when things cycle around, and he wanted to know how he's doing every three months to adjust based on politics, natural disasters, or whatever else might happen. Six months, he thought, was too long in today's economy.

"Look," he said to me, "at what's happened to the US economy over the last six months." At the time, he meant that the very conservative Donald Trump (whom I voted for 3 times) took over the presidency from the very liberal Joe Biden, causing a switch as big as when Biden took over from Trump four years earlier. Granted that switch might happen once every four or eight years, but politics is just one disruptive factor. Remember what Hurricane Katrina did to the oil rigs in the Gulf of Mexico? Remember the Dust Bowl back in the 1930s? Remember all the times the Mississippi flooded a million-plus acres of farmland?

It happened once, so it can—and probably will—happen again.

How often you meet with your financial advisors depends on your assets, your goals, and other factors. Just remember that *never* is *always* the wrong answer!

Your 30-Day Action Plan

In our initial meeting, we sit down with both spouses. I write out, on a whiteboard, our process and what it looks like to come on board, along with our expectations and fees. I put everything on the table and so by the time this discussion is done, it's absolutely clear whether we should move forward together or not.

I have all their information in front of me—assets, accounts, last year's tax return, and whatever else they have—and I draw out the structure of exactly what we do in our business. I explain that we don't start with investments but with risk management, and why we do it that way. Then I move to estate planning, shifting to talking about asset protection, acceleration, and legacy.

Then I move into what I call the "family office," a VAULT framework where we store all documents and financials so we have a living balance sheet of your life at all times. Only then do we move into investing, so that, by the end of the meeting, we all understand exactly where the whole process begins—with a solid foundation beneath the money. Asset managers typically begin with questions like: "Where's your money?" "How's it invested?" "Look at the allocations." Or, "Oh, I can get you another point or two," or "This has a better historical average." That's great stuff—but only in its proper time and place.

Everyone reading this book knows that, when you build a house, the town or county building inspectors check the contractors' work. They have to certify that everything meets code before you can move in. If the foundation or any other aspect of the build isn't done right, you'll have problems down the road, regardless of how well any specific contractor did their job. In fact, a bad foundation, plumbing, or wiring can damage work that others have done right. The same principle applies here. Many different skill sets contribute to financial security.

I may spend thirty or forty-five minutes—or more—up to this point talking about asset protection so the metaphorical house you've built is safe to live in. Then, metaphorically, we get to the renovation and expansion you want to add on. We believe this is a major differentiator between Pro Capital and other firms. I draw it out—a great visual that helps people understand the whole subject well enough to participate in their own financial future. Many of my clients sit through this meeting and say, "Thank you for that. That gives me a great deal to think about."

I'm a visual person, as most of us are. By drawing everything out on the board, I put your family's situation in front of you, adding more lines around it until we have a metaphorical steel-reinforced concrete vault—where creditors, lawsuits, divorces, or failing businesses can't penetrate to access your future security.

At that point, my question becomes, "Is this something you're looking for?"

The answer is usually a firm *yes!*

A Barrier

I mentioned earlier that if we bring you an investment or planning idea and you choose to move forward, we expect you to implement it through our firm.

Most people get that right away with no issue. Every now and then, though, I'll have someone say, *"Well, my buddy plays golf with another advisor every Thursday…"* That's fine. People naturally want to do business with those they know, like, and trust. But friendship doesn't always equal expertise. I've seen that go sideways, too.

So we're clear about our policy. We're not in the business of training our competition. I usually say it with a smile, but I mean it: *if you like our plan, great—implement it with us. If you'd rather take it to your golf buddy, that's fine too. But I'm not in the business of giving away the playbook for free.*

Most people laugh, nod, and move on. The right ones respect it because they know professionals value professionalism. At the end of the day, clear expectations build trust faster than any friendship ever could.

The Next Step

Timeline	Focus & Action Steps
Week 1 – Clarify Your Vision	• Define your three-generation wealth goals in writing. • Have the "money conversation" with your spouse and children. • Identify your top three wealth-protection concerns.

Week 2 – Audit Your Vulnerabilities	• List all assets and how they're titled. • Review all insurance coverage for gaps. • Examine business partnership agreements and liability exposures.
Week 3 – Document Your System	• Collect paperwork on all income streams and assess stability. • Review or create your investment policies and procedures. • Determine if your wealth could be managed without you.
Week 4 – Evaluate Your Professional Team	• Meet with your CPA, attorney, and insurance agent. • Ask each: "What are the biggest risks you see in my financial situation?" • Determine if your advisors are coordinating with one another.

I've seen plenty of people with great intentions get stuck in neutral—always planning, rarely moving. This thirty-day step is how we break that cycle. It's about creating movement, not perfection. Like a doctor, I can give you the diagnosis and the prescription, but the healing only happens when you follow through. Take action, get it done, and you'll build momentum that changes everything.

The Hard Truth

Most people don't want to hear that you can't DIY comprehensive wealth planning.

Technically, you can. Millions are doing it—but are those millions also planning to do a root canal on their kids or a little corrective surgery maybe? No, they leave that to professionals.

Yes, it costs money to hire professionals—and extra to hire good ones. But here's the math: the average Pro Capital client discovers hidden opportunities within their first year of working with us. Those opportunities include tax savings, insurance customization, investment improvements, and estate planning efficiencies.

Whether you're a carpenter or an engineer, you don't give your skills away. You spent time, effort, and (in most cases) a lot of money building your skill set. You don't expect to give those skills away, so why would you expect others to?

Likewise, your time is worth more to you, in the long run, being used to build your business.

The Assessment that Changed Everything

The "Johnson" family came to us worth about $13 million. They were successful business owners in their fifties—good people who thought they had everything handled. Their VAULT Assessment revealed:

- $2.3 million in unnecessary estate tax exposure
- Zero asset protection despite a significant liability risk
- An investment portfolio with forty percent overlap and massive tax inefficiency
- Life insurance beneficiaries that were nonexistent
- No business succession plan despite having two children in the business

Within 18 months of implementing our recommendations:

- Their estate tax exposure was eliminated

- Their assets were protected with comprehensive liability shields
- Their investment efficiency improved, generating more cash flow than before
- Their insurance improved with the same coverage at a lower cost
- A business succession plan was in place, including a family buy-in

Their total investment in professional planning was $75,000, but the total value added to their assets was $3.2 million. Their return on investment was 4,267 percent, meaning that for every dollar they invested with us, we helped them create over $400 in real, usable wealth.

The Johnsons now have greater confidence. Their children understand the family wealth plan and active participants in it. Their business is protected. Their legacy is secure. More importantly, they have the peace of mind to focus on what they love: running their business and enjoying their family.

Example is for illustrative purposes only. Actual results will vary and may be more or less favorable.

A Decision Every Successful Person Eventually Makes

At some point, every high-performing individual reaches a crossroads—not driven by fear, but by responsibility and intentionality. There are two paths forward:

Option 1: Maintain Your Current Approach

Continue with your existing structure and relationships. Rely on the systems you already have in place and revisit planning only as circumstances change. This approach works for many people–particularly when finances are straightforward and risks are minimal.

Option 2: Take a More Integrated, Proactive Approach

Engage in a comprehensive assessment of your financial picture. Coordinate strategy across investments, taxes, protection, and legacy planning. Put systems in place designed to support long-term clarity, efficiency, and adaptability as your life and wealth evolve.

Getting Started: The Pro Capital Process

The real question isn't whether comprehensive planning is necessary for everyone. It's whether a more intentional, coordinated approach aligns with the level of success and responsibility you've achieved.

As the old proverb says:

"Failing to plan is planning to fail."

A more modern truth might be this:

Your future outcomes are shaped by the decisions you're willing to make today.

Summary

If you're ready to move beyond scattered planning to systematic wealth protection, here's how we work:

Initial Consultation (90 minutes)
Complete a VAULT Assessment using the methodology described in this chapter. We look to identify vulnerabilities and opportunities specific to your situation.

Analysis (2 to 3 weeks):
Our team conducts a comprehensive analysis of your current situation, creates financial models, and develops recommendations.

Presentation (2 hours)
We present our findings and strategic recommendations, including specific implementation timelines and projected outcomes.

Implementation (3 to 6 months)
Systematic execution of approved strategies, with regular progress updates and coordination with your existing professional team.

Ongoing
Semi-annual reviews and annual comprehensive assessments to ensure your VAULT remains on track as your wealth and circumstances evolve.

The journey from scattered planning to systematic wealth protection begins with a single decision: are you ready to stop hoping for the best and start creating it?

CHAPTER 11

Building the Bench

Fundamental Ideas:

1. A synergistic team of professionals is your best road to success.
2. *Professional* is not a job title–it's an attitude.

Assemble Professionals Who Multiply Your Money

Just like an NFL team needs players and plays coordinated by a team of coaches–with one head coach–wealth building requires a coordinated, professional team.

I've been around a lot of egos in my life. When egos start getting in the way of a team working together, winning breaks down. The point of a head-coach approach is *not* to make anyone look bad. That job exists to coordinate the team. Chaos ensues when professionals don't work together and let their egos dominate their lives. There was an instance in which we found $1.5 million that wasn't on the books because the accountant and attorney didn't know about those assets. (Or wouldn't admit that they knew but did nothing.)

On the flip side, when professionals are aligned, awesome stuff happens. With tax and legal changes coming every year, the industries evolve to the point where new opportunities appear–opportunities that can either profit you or hurt you.

If everyone doesn't maintain a team attitude, it ends badly or, at the very least, opportunities are missed.

Each professional in your financial ecosystem will have specific, documented roles and responsibilities.

What Makes a Professional?

Before winning fame as the creator of *Star Trek,* Gene Roddenberry, while still serving as a Los Angeles police officer, published an article in *The Beat* describing "seven basic obligations" of a professional–principles of duty, discipline, and service (Alexander, *Star Trek Creator*, 66-67).

1. A duty to serve mankind generally rather than self, individuals or groups.

2. A duty to prepare as fully as practicable for services before entering active practice.

3. A duty to continually work to improve skills by all means available and to freely communicate professional information gained.

4. A duty to employ full skill at all times regardless of considerations of personal gain, comfort or safety, and at all times to assist fellow professionals upon demand.

5. A duty to regulate practice by the franchising of practitioners, setting the highest practicable intellectual and technical minimums; to accept and upgrade fellow professionals solely upon considerations of merit; and to be constantly alert to protect society from fraudulent, substandard or unethical practice through ready and swift disenfranchisement.

6. A duty to zealously guard the honor of the profession by living exemplary lives publicly and privately, recognizing that injury to a group serving society injures society.

7. A duty to give constant attention to the improvement of self-discipline, recognizing that the individual must be the master of himself to be the servant of others.
    —Quoted in *Star Trek Creator* by David Alexander

Gene and I might disagree on the details, but the essential value—duty—I wholeheartedly approve of. Professionalism is core to success in financial management. Our jobs, if done poorly, can ruin lives; if done well, they can extend freedom. Your professional financial management team should include:

Role	Primary Function	Key Responsibilities	Analogy / Perspective
Wealth Manager/ Financial Director – "The CFO"	Leads and coordinates the overall planning team; serves as the client's central strategist.	• Create and manage comprehensive balance sheets. • Identify tax savings opportunities. • Adjust portfolios for risk management. • Ensure proper titling of all assets. • Direct systems to prevent orphaned or lost assets.	Like a house manager in an old English estate— overseeing all moving parts, maintaining order, and standing guard against blind spots, gaps, or changes that could threaten the household.

Tax Professional – "A Forward Planner"	Anticipates future tax outcomes and strategies, not just annual filings.	• Multi-year tax projections to prevent surprises. • Estimated payment and cash-flow planning. • Deduction management and payment mitigation. • Advises other team members on tax implications.	Goes beyond filing forms—thinks years ahead so clients never face an unexpected tax bill.
Estate Planning Attorney – "A Specialist in Passing On"	Designs the legal framework for generational wealth transfer and probate avoidance.	• Trust and estate structuring. • Asset protection integration. • Multi-generational and charitable planning. • Business succession strategy.	Protects legacy from public exposure and legal inefficiency—ensures wealth passes quietly, cleanly, and intentionally.
Business Attorney – "An Entity Architect"	Builds and maintains the legal walls protecting business and personal assets.	• Optimize entity structure (LLC, S-Corp, C-Corp, etc.). • Draft operating agreements. • Create business protection and separation strategies. • Coordinate exit, sale, or retirement planning.	Like an architect, designing the blueprint for the business's legal foundation and longevity.

Insurance Specialist – "A Risk Transfer Expert"	Mitigates exposure through coordinated insurance strategy across personal and business interests.	• Conduct comprehensive risk assessments. • Structure insurance for asset protection. • Ensure estate liquidity for taxes and settlements. • Plan for long-term care and disability risks.	Converts unpredictable risks into predictable costs—protecting everything you've built when life happens.

Avoid Common Mistakes

As I mentioned in the previous chapter, we filter clients and we're not afraid to say, "If that's you, you're not made to work with us." Better to walk away than to get stuck with a grief-factory.

The "God Complex"

It's a challenge most people have seen, and many have dealt with. Attorneys and doctors are notorious for thinking they're superior to other mere mortals. It reminds me of the old joke, "Those who think they know it all only annoy those of us who do."

Among the warning signs are professional opinions coated with personal bias; attempts to sell their product based solely on their own assurances; a failure to listen to family goals; a desire to control everything; and arrogant attitudes that assume they're better than the client.

These attitudes have costs. When egos clash, people stop talking, things get missed, and problems arise. It also encourages the price shopping "trap." Practitioners suffering from the god complex often overcharge for their opinions; this, in turn, encourages the public to look for good deals. Granted, there are practitioners who don't overcharge, but would you choose a plastic surgeon exclusively because he or she is the cheapest? Would you fly to Mexico on a cheap, no-name airline?

Investing in quality professionals can save exponentially more than they cost. Think about it this way: if we can project saving hundreds of thousands–or millions–in future taxes and lawsuit protection, then ask you to pay us $50,000 for that proper plan, are we not worth our fee? In that respect, it's no different than the insurance you willingly pay for on your life, health, home, or car.

Credential Confusion

Credentials are great, but they don't guarantee real-world success. Credentials mean studies done, exams passed, licenses obtained–that's all. They don't promise that the "credentialed expert" really knows what he or she is talking about. For example, inherited assets in Texas are, technically, separate property protected in a divorce. In reality, I've seen plenty of divorce cases in which inherited property (those same inherited assets) was divided equally.

There can also be a gap between the law on paper (statutes on the books) and real-life experience (what's best for all concerned). Many cases are decided strictly on facts–the letter of the law. Many are not so cut-and-dried; they must be judged on the spirit of the law. As an old sage once said, "You can't live the spirit of the law until you understand and live the letter of the law." Living the spirit of the law requires people who've actually lived it. (I know, that sounds so simple it shouldn't need to be said, but it does.) Nothing trumps actual experience navigating difficult situations.

And, while we're on this subject, slick marketing doesn't translate to competence, either.

Conflicts-of-Interest

In a true professional, the clients' goals come first. Sales trainer and motivational speaker Zig Ziglar said it best:

> You can have everything in life you want, if you will just help other people get what they want.
> —*Secrets of Closing the Sale*, 1984

At Pro Capital, we protect and grow assets. We're a personal service company, how can we say we're successful if you aren't? In all our dealings with other professionals, if we don't share the same goal, then we have nothing to talk about.

One of the "god complex" red flags are the so-called professionals who push their agenda instead of clients' goals. Ensure every member of your team is aligned with you and that your goals are their goals for you before you move forward with them.

Communication and Coordination Gaps

The biggest problems we see are uncoordinated team members, such situations are inefficient and confusing. That can lead to a killer—blind spots and gaps in coverage. The CFO needs to carefully coordinate work so that everything gets done, and it only gets done once. To eliminate this, everyone must be onboard with communicating and coordinating; regular reports must be submitted and distributed so all tasks are documented; and team pros must be responsive to those requests and reports.

Team pros must exhibit a "no problem" attitude when working together: "No problem, I'll get that handled," or "No problem, he's/she's the best person to get that done." Check the egos at the door. If you see red flags rising, like nonresponsive professionals or bozos who won't "play nice" with the team, these people need to get kicked off the team immediately. If not, there are real-world impacts: assets get lost. Opportunities get missed. Problems creep in and take up residence.

Implementation: Building Your Team

Phase	Key Actions
Assessment Phase	• Use the Professional Team Building Checklist appended to this chapter to evaluate your current team. • Identify gaps in personnel and process. • Review and/or replace individuals via a professional reference and vetting system.
Integration Phase	• Host an initial team meeting for introductions, coordination, and to explain duties and expectations. • Establish communications protocols and schedules, including reporting standards. • Schedule ongoing review and management meetings.

Maintenance Phase	• Host regular team review meetings or retreats–annually is usually sufficient. • Hold individual performance measurement interviews, ideally before major review meetings. • Adjust the team roster as needs evolve.

The Pro Capital Difference

We've found the CFO coordination model to be very effective. Using the client's Vision & Values statement as "the page," the CFO gets everyone on that page and keeps them there. We understand the need for documentation with everything, ensuring all strategies are properly recorded and titled. We hold to the old proverb, "If it isn't written down, it didn't happen."

We understand that clients engage us to stand guard over their assets. We're always watching–constantly vigilant for emerging risks, with an eagle eye open for new opportunities. In this, we agree wholeheartedly with the old saying, "There are three kinds of people in the world: those who make things happen; those who watch things happen; and those who wonder what happened." We aim to be the first–proactive in all we do–instead of being reactive or inactive.

Our years of experience have taught us to identify blind spots that others miss, and there have been a lot of those. We've seen generational wealth disappear and become keenly aware of the need for multi-generational planning to secure that wealth in a family-focused protection plan. Ongoing oversight and management have become second nature to us.

We utilize a flexible review schedule and give clients the choice in how often we meet and review. Our standard is a semi-annual review for families, but we understand that some feel a need for monthly check-ins while others prefer a "don't call me unless something's wrong" scenario. We respect client preferences because we understand that no two clients' needs are the same. Some do need continuous monitoring, so we constantly watch the trajectory, ready to make needed tweaks while, for others, small adjustments (minor course corrections) can be covered or authorized as part of the client agreement.

We've assembled a quality team through a strict selection criterion. Each is a specialist, a professional expert in their field. Each was committed to the team-player philosophy before they came to us. They're also goal-oriented and focused on client outcomes. Each has experience with high-net-worth clients and understands the complexities of significant wealth.

I said early on that when I wasn't drafted, it told me what the League thought of me: I wasn't "destined" to be a Pro Bowl or Hall of Fame player. When I got lucky and signed a contract, I knew I had to listen harder, train harder, and work harder than other players if I wanted to make it—even to a second season.

So, every time I walked onto an NFL field, I knew my job and did it. In a world where you're usually a has-been after three years, I lasted six and could have lasted longer if not for events beyond my control. I was one of the lucky 17,000 out of one million who wore a pro jersey that I didn't buy in a souvenir shop.

I really was a *professional* football player. I saw a lot of guys who weren't. The differences I saw set the pattern for the rest of my working life.

On any team, every player must know their role, execute their assignment, and work toward the common goal under the direction of the head coach. The question isn't whether you can afford to build a world-class professional team. The question is: how much will you lose if you don't?

CHAPTER 12

BUILT FOR FREEDOM

Fundamental Ideas:

1. This is who we are: builders, protectors, and planners. If you've made it this far, you're probably one of us. Let's keep the conversation going at *ProCapitalTX.com*.

2. This book is a challenge. If you see yourself in these pages, act on it. If you don't, that's fine, just don't sit still.

3. Conviction separates talkers from doers. I made my choice years ago, and now it's your turn.

4. We reject the victim mindset. Ownership is the only path to real power, and that starts with personal responsibility.

5. I'm not here to sugarcoat, I'm here to prepare. Face the hard truths, build systems around them, and stay ready when life hits back.

From Test to Testimony: The Entrepreneurial Journey

How I Came to Believe What I Believe about Money

I began this book with my personal story. My introduction to the realities of family wealth building and protection came at seventeen, when I had an auto accident that severely damaged my family's financial health. My parents' multiple marriages and divorces had also damaged our family's financial health, taught me about the law of unintended consequences, and brought to my attention how ungenerous some people could be, even to family. I got through college and into the NFL and saw real wealth for the first time. I also saw how stupidly some people spend their money. Few NFL players come from wealthy families; we played because we loved the game, and because it gave us a shot at more money than anything else we could do.

After my career-ending injury, I wanted to keep playing, and I could have, but business considerations outweighed personal relationships and, at age twenty-eight, I was a "has-been." Shortly after, I got married and had to worry about a family instead of myself alone. I quickly saw that other jobs with the team would demand a family sacrifice that I wasn't willing to make. After a while, I saw a need to take better control my own finances which led me to my present profession. Along this journey, I learned several truths:

- **The Reality of Building Wealth:** America now boasts over six million families with investable assets above $1 million—millionaires. Estimates vary, but at least three-quarters of them are self-made.
- **Passing Down the Story:** Almost three out of four wealthy families lose that wealth by the second generation; nine out of ten by the third.
- **Values Transfer:** Most family financial disasters are predictable—illness, accidents, lawsuits, economic downturns, and more—therefore, they are preventable or mitigatable.
- **Preventing Entitlement:** Demanding that our children earn what they have is good parenting; it preserves the hunger and appreciation of success.

Thomas Paine (in *The American Crisis*) rightly said, "What we obtain too cheaply we esteem too lightly."

The True Definition of Financial Freedom

Conventional wisdom measures wealth in numbers: your bank balance, the dollar value of your value assets, the number of cars, houses, and other things you own, and so on.

Real wisdom measures wealth in time—that is, the freedom to use your time as you choose: the time you invest in a project versus the dollars returned; time spent with family instead of punching a clock or drawing a salary; and time spent giving service to your community, church, or neighbors.

A comfortable lifestyle is something everybody wants. One of the biggest lies of 21st-century America is that lifestyle is more important than life. Too many live beyond their means, enslaved to a lifestyle they can't afford instead of living the life they choose.

In other words, freedom is having options—the ability to choose in good times and in bad times. Financial freedom makes bad times easier and preserves your options during those hard times.

The Ultimate Choice

The choice now before you confronts us all—be built or be broke; be wealthy or be poor; live a life of abundance or scarcity.

The potential harvest is bountiful, but willing laborers are few. The world is bursting with opportunity, but too many people are unwilling to do what it takes to obtain the bounty or to make sure that their legacy passes down to their children and beyond. Even though the knowledge is readily available and the tools are waiting in the box, too many put it off until a tomorrow that never comes.

Freedom in Crisis: Being Present When It Matters Most

When my stepdad, Charlie, passed away, I was able to simply *be there* for my mom. As her son, I believed that was my job, to show up fully during one of the hardest moments of her life. Because of financial freedom, I could do that. I wasn't tied to a 9-to-5 job or a boss demanding I stay in a chair while life happened outside of it. I called the office and said, "I won't be in. Cancel all my meetings. Reschedule everything." And that's exactly what my team did. Anyone who didn't understand that wasn't meant to be part of my world.

That's what financial freedom truly gives you: *confidence and permission to move when life moves.* It's the ability to serve the people you love most when they need you most, without checking a calendar or asking for approval. My freedom didn't erase my mom's grief, but it gave me the chance to be the son she needed in that moment. That eased her burden, and that matters.

Financial freedom doesn't just change what you can buy; it changes who you can *be* when it counts. It removes the need to ask permission to prioritize what's sacred. It gives you the privilege of availability—the ability to cancel everything and still be right where you're supposed to be.

And in moments like that, you find out which business relationships truly value humanity over hustle.

Generational Choices: The Stay-at-Home Parent Decision

When we had our babies, my wife decided she wanted to be a stay-at-home mom. I was grateful for that desire. I said, "No problem at all," because I wanted that same opportunity for her and for them while they were young. We didn't want to hand them off to have someone in a daycare center raise our kids. We wanted to raise them ourselves.

That decision has generational impact. We could cite studies all day long about the benefits of having a parent at home, but our decision wasn't academic—it was personal! Financial freedom allowed Megan to stay home while I continued working. Every decision about our kids was made by us, not forced on us by outside circumstances or the demands of a perceived lifestyle.

We understood that parental presence in early childhood creates lasting family bonds. It removed competition. We chose to be the primary influence in children's lives rather than defaulting to external caregivers. We recognized that time with young children is a non-renewable resource, and it passes far too quickly!

More Generational Choices: The Great-Grandchildren Question

The legacy you leave is what your great-grandchildren will thank you for. It's beating that ninety percent probability and bringing your wealth creation full circle so your children and grandchildren can have the life you worked to set up for them.

I want mine to see the work I put into becoming an NFL player. I want them to see that because I had a bit of a fear-based mindset early in life from the wreck, I appreciated and cared for my money when it came. I want them to see that I held on to my money instead of spending it impulsively. I want them to see that I created a new career and a wealth-building system. I want them to see that I have the testimony that comes from the test—from that first and the subsequent personal crises in my life—that I must help entrepreneurial families build wealth and legacy.

Which begs the question: what will your great-grandchildren say about your financial decisions? Are they going to thank you? Will they even know your name? Ultimately, I think it would be pretty amazing to live a life that is known one hundred years after our time on this planet.

Community and Calling: Freedom to Serve Beyond Yourself

Our financial freedom also allowed us freedom to work with our church and with nonprofits, and to get to know the neighbors in our community and build real relationships with them. I still get up early and stay late at work, doing things only I can do (being the boss). But on the days I didn't have to—or the days I chose not to—if I saw a neighbor, I could take the time to get to know them. By doing that, we've been able to help develop a community around us, a community of people who enjoy spending time with each other and speaking into their lives.

One other thing to point out: ours is an affluent neighborhood. Our financial freedom contributes to theirs, and theirs to ours, by creating a community that serves as a haven from "the world." This allows us to set aside many everyday stresses so we can tackle tomorrow in the best physical and mental shape. (That always adds to your probability of success.) As Australian mining tycoon Lang Hancock reportedly said, "The best way to help poor people is not to be one of them."

The Calling Component: Freedom to Focus Above

Not everyone believes God has a plan for us; some don't believe He exists at all. For the rest of us, aligning financial structure with spiritual calling helps us to focus on the important things of life here and hereafter. Economic freedom brings a clearer, stronger focus on our purposes. Remember the parable of rich fool in Luke 12? His land produced abundantly, and he said to himself that he would tear down his barns and build bigger ones to store his grain and goods. He planned to relax, eat, drink, and enjoy life. But that very night, God told him his time on Earth was over. This is the ultimate train wreck scenario. What good, at that moment, were all his goods to him?

The VAULT Method in Action: The Ripple Effect

The VAULT Method exists to protect wealth. Use it to create a metaphorical vault so that when (not if) disaster strikes, your wealth can't be touched, taken, or taxed away. It creates income streams that outlast your lifetime—legacies that grow for generations and financial peace that lets you focus on what matters most.

VAULT helps us define a family vision. When that vision is clear, it creates an incredible ripple effect. Families who have struggled to define what they wanted to do with their wealth gain clarity. Within the VAULT, they set long-term and interim goals, giving them a picture of their future and a roadmap to get there.

They also learn the language they need to communicate well—not just internally, but to their families. Because of that, Thanksgiving dinner (a metaphor for family relationships) ceases to be a source of tension. It becomes a true celebration—a time to look forward to discussing every aspect of the family's future, because VAULT requires openness about money. Once that great hurdle is overcome, the rest generally flows like a mountain stream.

Our own success in establishing financial freedom encourages us to reach out to those in need. Imagine the joy you feel driving home from taking a dinner to a family or families who've been hit by some trial or tribulation. Such acts of charity help others through tough times and remind us of the gifts God has freely bestowed on us. They teach our children and other families how interconnected all of us are. Such acts of kindness ultimately help increase the movement to become creators and protectors of wealth so that they, too, can be of greater service to others.

Consider how these ideas could contribute to rippling the effects of your financial strength:

- **The Judeo-Christian Framework:** operate from a foundation of traditional (historically successful) values and long-term thinking.
- **See Client Relationships as Friendships:** share your visions and values to create lasting bonds and expand your sphere of influence

- **Establish a Referral Culture:** you have people you trust; others seek trustworthy people–it's a match made in heaven.
- **Articulation Power:** remember, "We should not write so that it is possible for the reader to understand us, but so that it is impossible for him to misunderstand us" (Quintilian, Roman educator, 1 AD), and you'll develop the ability to clearly communicate your mission and attract aligned clients

How Free Are You?

Ask yourself some questions:

- Can I miss work for two weeks without asking permission?
- Can my spouse stay home with our children without financial stress?
- Can I say yes to meaningful service opportunities without checking the cost?
- Can I be generous without worrying about providing for my own family?

The Last Words: Choosing Rich versus Wrecked

Most Decisions Boil Down to Binary Choices

- Rich versus Wrecked: do you want to have and protect assets?
- Wealthy versus Poor: is your mind focused on plenty or scarcity?
- Emotion versus Logic: do you operate from emotion (fear) or from logic (faith)?

- Your Daily Choice: how will what I do today move my family toward the outcomes we desire?

Principles of the Harvest

- The World's Abundance: God created a world with enough—and to spare—for all His children.
- Be Willing: many are called but few are chosen, and those who are not chosen are often not because they were excluded, but because they chose not to do the things that lead to success.
- Plentiful Opportunity: opportunities abound for those prepared to see them.
- The Action Gap: bridge the space between knowing and doing by looking for opportunities and taking advantage of them.
- You Don't Have to Reinvent the Wheel: we know how to succeed and have systems in place to do so, you just have to learn them and execute them.
- Implementation versus Procrastination: the difference between "today" and "someday" thinking.
- Overcoming the Averages: realize that statistics apply to the masses; your individual outcomes are based almost entirely on your choices.

Built for Impact

Why I Wrote This Book

I've spent my life in locker rooms, boardrooms, and client meetings. The settings changed, but the lesson stayed the same: the win always goes to those who prepare, stay disciplined, and surround themselves with the right team. *Built, Not Broke* was born out of that belief. It's the playbook I wish more families had—one that ties financial systems to purpose, protection, and legacy. Because money without meaning isn't freedom. It's just noise.

The Megaphone of Money

Money is a tool, pure and simple. It's not good or bad; it just amplifies who you already are.

If you're selfish, money makes you louder about it. If you're generous, money expands your reach.

People often say, *"Money changed them."* The truth? It didn't. Money just revealed who they were all along.

Our mission is to help high-character entrepreneurs amplify the right things: generosity, wisdom, and legacy, so their wealth builds both lives and lineages.

Some Great Reads That Shaped My Thinking

Great leaders are lifelong learners. These books each played a part in how I think about wealth, values, and business:

- *Rich Dad Poor Dad* by Robert Kiyosaki—Foundational thinking about cash flow and mindset.
- *The Big Retirement Risk* by Erin Botsford—My mentor's blueprint for retiring with control, not fear.
- *Poverty, Riches & Wealth* by Kris Vallotton—An incredible perspective on the spiritual and moral side of abundance.
- *Made in America* by Sam Walton—The story of a humble visionary who built empires through grit, service, and faith.

These authors all proved something powerful: you don't have to know everything. You just need the right values, the right team, and the courage to execute.

Join the Movement

If this book resonated with you, I'd love to stay connected. Visit **ProCapitalTX.com** to:

- Download tools and resources mentioned in this book.
- Subscribe to our newsletter.
- Set a goals call with our team.

Final Word

I hope this book showed you more than just strategies. I hope you saw the values that shaped me: discipline, perseverance, and integrity—and how those same values build lasting wealth.

Wealth isn't about luck. It's about building with intention. It's about standing guard over what matters, protecting your people, and laying foundations strong enough for the next generation to keep building on.

That's the mindset of every builder who refuses to quit. It's the difference between being broke by circumstance and *built by design.*

Built. Not Broke.

Appendices

APPENDIX 1

Practical Tools Exercise

Tool 1, Step 1: Apply Maslow's Hierarchy

Dr. Maslow defined five levels of needs:

1. Physiological (food, clothing, shelter).
2. Safety (protection from clear and present dangers).
3. Love & Belonging (social connections).
4. Self-esteem (achieving your goals).
5. Self-actualization (achieving your dreams).

Let's look at translating those concepts to financial planning. Remember, this is a pyramid with physiological needs at the bottom. If you're worried about where your next meal is coming from, you're not interested in joining the local book club.

1. Vitals (Basic Living Expenses)

What income do I require to function?

- Housing (rent/mortgage): $ __________/month.
- Food & Utilities: $ __________/month.
- Clothing: $ __________/month.

- Transportation[A]: $ __________/month.
- Healthcare[B]: $ __________/month.
- Minimum Debt Payments: $ __________/month.
- Total Vital Expense: $ __________/month.

Notes:

[A] Includes auto insurance, repairs, etc.

[B] Includes insurance protection, maybe a gym membership.

- Basic Health: $ __________/month.
- Disability: $ __________/month.
- Life: $ __________/month.
- Long-term Care[C]: $ __________/month.

Insurance is *non-negotiable*. As a man, if you have a spouse, children, or grandchildren depending on you, life insurance isn't optional. It's your job as a husband and father. There's a harsh reality in that industry; we've had to tell people they're uninsurable and when it's needed most is when you can't get it. You owe your family every possible protection. Don't leave them financially devastated.

[C] Long-Term Care, the hidden threat that can cost $400,000-plus per year for quality care.

- The risk: without planning, it can wipe out a lifetime of wealth.
- The solution: insurance transfers this massive financial risk.

2. Lifestyle

What income do I require to maintain my standard of living?

- Entertainment: $ ___________/month.
- Nice Restaurants: $ ___________/month.
- Quality Clothing: $ ___________/month.
- Hobbies: $ ___________/month.
- Continuing Education: $ ___________/month.
- Total Lifestyle Expenses: $ ___________/month.

3. Wants

What income do I require to feel like I've done right by others?

- Charitable Giving: $ ___________/month.
- Children's Education $ ___________/month.
- Debt Repayment: $ ___________/month.
- Total Wants Expense: $ ___________/month.

4. Wishes

What income do I require to feel rich?

- Boat: $ ___________/month.
- Country Club: $ ___________/month.
- Vacations: $ ___________/month.
- Total Wishes Expense: $ ___________/month.

5. Dreams

What income do I require to leave a lasting legacy for the world?

- The Bucket List: $ ___________/month.
- Family Foundation: $ ___________/month.
- Total Dreams Expense: $ ___________/month.

Tool 1, Step 2: Calculate your After-Tax Income Gap

Important: Calculate your income needs *after* taxes, especially if withdrawing from tax-deferred accounts like IRAs and 401(k)s.

Monthly After-tax Income Needs

- Vitals: $ ___________/month.
- Lifestyle: $ ___________/month.
- Wants: $ ___________/month.
- Wishes: $ ___________/month.
- Total Monthly: $ ___________/month.
- Total Annual: $ ___________/year.

If your estimated tax rate on withdrawals equals X%, then the pre-tax income needed is after tax income divided by one minus the tax rate. For example.

If you need $100,000 income with an after-tax rate of twenty-five percent, your pre-tax need is $100,000 ÷ 0.75 = $133,333.

Guaranteed Income Sources (After-Tax $)

- Social Security: $ ___________/month.
- Pensions: $ ___________/month.
- Other: $ ___________/month.
- Total Guaranteed: $ ___________/month.
- Gap to Fill: $ ___________/month.
- Pre-Tax Gap Needed: $ ___________/year.

Tool 2: The Business Exit Income Planner

(For business owners planning to sell or sunset)

Current Situation

- Business income: $ ___________/year.
- Personal expenses: $ ___________/year.
- Current savings rate: $ ___________/year.

Post-Business Scenario

- Sale proceeds (estimated): $ ___________.
- Tax on sale (estimated): $ ___________.
- Net proceeds available: $ ___________.

Retirement Income Plan

Annual expenses needed after-taxes

- Social Security (estimated): $ ___________/year.
- Income gap to fill: $ ___________/year.

Required Investment Capital

4% withdrawal rule: Gap ÷ 0.04 = $ ___________.
5% withdrawal rule: Gap ÷ 0.05 = $ ___________.

Reality Check
- Net sale proceeds: $______/month.
- Required capital: $______/month.
- Surplus/Shortfall: $______/month.

Tool 3: The Market Disaster Test

For each investment, ask:
1. If the market drops fifty percent, does this still pay me?
2. Which aspects of your income can be cut?
3. Which aspects of your income can be eliminated?
4. Do I need to sell stocks or liquidate other assets to get income?
5. How long can I wait for recovery?

Tool 4: The Three-Category Portfolio Allocator

Total Investable Assets: $______/month.
- SPG (30-40%): $______/month.
- Hybrids (40-50%): $______/month.
- Growth Funds (10-20%): $______/month.

Income Check
- SPG: $______/year.
- Hybrid: $______/year.
- Growth: $______/year.
- Portfolio Total: $______/year.

Your Goal
A portfolio income that's greater than after-tax income gap.

LEGACY PLANNING TOOLS

1. The Estate Tax Impact Calculator

- Your Current Net Worth: $
- Federal Exemption (2024): $ 13,610,000
- Taxable Amount (Federal): $ _______________
- Federal Estate Tax (40%): $ _______________

- Your State: ___________.
- Taxable Amount (State): $ _______________
- State Estate Tax: $ _______________
- State Inheritance Tax: $ _______________

- Taxes Paid: $ _______________
- Left for Family: $ _______________

2. The Three D's Planning Checklist

Death Planning

- Current will (updated every three years or when major life changes occur).
- Trust documents properly executed and funded.
- Estate tax minimization planned.
- Business succession plan enacted.
- Life insurance for estate liquidity paid up.
- Charitable giving strategy defined.

Disability Planning

- Financial power of attorney signed and sealed.
- Healthcare power of attorney signed and sealed.
- Living will/healthcare directives signed and sealed.
- Disability insurance coverage paid up.
- Business continuity procedures signed and sealed.
- Successor trustee named and notified.

Divorce Protection

- Prenuptial/postnuptial agreements signed and sealed.
- Asset protection trust structures signed and sealed.
- Business ownership safeguards in place and key players informed.
- Separate property documentation signed and sealed.
- Beneficiary protections in trusts signed and sealed.

3. Asset Titling Audit–Review How Each Major Asset Is Currently Owned

Primary Residence:

- Value: $ __________
- Current Owner: __________
- Recommended: __________

Investment Accounts

- Value: $ __________
- Current Owner: __________
- Recommended: __________

Business Ownership
- Value: $ _____________
- Current Owner: _____________
- Recommended: _____________

Life Insurance
- Value: $ _____________
- Current Owner: _____________
- Recommended: _____________

Retirement Accounts (401(k) or IRA)
- Value: $ _____________
- 1st Beneficiary: _____________
- 2nd Beneficiary: _____________

Red Flag Double Check List
- Is ownership in your personal name?
- Are all beneficiaries named on all accounts?
- Is the ex-spouse still listed anywhere?
- Are contingent beneficiaries named?
- Is the trust established and properly funded?
- Does the business have a succession plan?

4. Legacy Goals Assessment

Take these steps to determine your strategy progress.

1. Control the Priorities

- You keep control until your death.
- You can start transferring control now.
- You must maintain some control and share some.

2. Family Beneficiary Options

- Spouse first then children.
- Children directly, spouse separately.
- Grandchildren, step-children, others.
- Any future generations.

3. Charitable Options

- None, the heirs get it all.
- Some to charity, the family gets most.
- Significant charitable legacy, the family gets some.
- A specific amount to charity: $ ___________

4. Privacy Options

- Probate is a public spectacle, engaging a trust can safeguard your privacy.
- Some is needed but you generally don't care who knows what.
- If you absolutely don't care about privacy, a simple will suffice.

5. Tax Minimization

- It's your right to minimize any taxes you might have to pay.
- It's a civic duty to keep the government from taking more than absolutely necessary.
- Paying some tax inclines the government to not investigate as deeply as they might.

6. Business Future Options

- The family takes over.
- Key employees buy you out.
- Sell to outsiders.

No succession plan might mean the loss of the business and the livelihoods of all your employees.

5. Assemble a Professional Team

1. Your Legacy Planning Team

- Business Attorney (handles succession planning).
- Business Valuation Expert (determines fair market value).
- Estate Planning Attorney (licensed in your state).
- Financial Advisor (coordinates overall strategy).
- Life Insurance Specialist (designs insurance strategies).
- Tax Advisor/CPA (experienced with estates).

2. Team Coordination Questions

- Do all the professionals communicate with each other?
- Is there a committee chair coordinating everything?
- Are they all updated on your current situation?
- Do they understand your family's values and goals?

Warning: State Laws Vary Significantly!

3. States with Favorable Trust Laws:

Alaska, Delaware, Nevada, South Dakota.

4. States with High Estate Taxes:

Connecticut, Massachusetts, New York.

Remember, every state can change their statutes every time their legislature meets!

The Bottom Line Is Your Money's Final Destination

When you die, every dollar you have will go to one of three places.

1. Your Family

- Requires proper planning.
- Bequests can be structured to protect and motivate kids.

2. The Government

- Federal estate tax is forty percent.
- State taxes (where they apply) vary from twelve to twenty percent.
- Inheritance taxes (where they apply) vary from two to sixteen percent.
- Income tax on retirement accounts could total over one-third of the value of your estate.
- Without planning, the government could take more than half of your wealth.

3. Charity(ies)

- Can be part of your legacy plan.
- Provides tax benefits.
- Reduces what government gets.

PROFESSIONAL TEAM BUILDING CHECKLIST

Your Guide to Assembling a Championship Wealth Team

The Team-Building Checklist

Wealth Manager/Financial Director

Key Questions to Ask:

1. "How do you coordinate with other professionals on my team?"

Look for: specific process, regular communication, team meeting facilitation.

2. "Walk me through how you manage a client's complete balance sheet."

Look for: comprehensive tracking, asset titling oversight, gap identification.

3. "Tell me about a time you found a significant oversight in a client's financial picture."

Look for: real examples, proactive discovery, quantifiable impact.

4. "How do you ensure nothing falls through the cracks?"

Look for: systematic approach, documentation processes, regular reviews.

Must-Have Capabilities:
- Balance sheet creation and management
- Tax management strategy coordination
- Asset titling oversight ("titling supersedes every-thing")
- Risk management integration
- Multi-professional team coordination experience
- Documentation and tracking systems

Red Flags:
- Only focuses on investments, ignores the broader picture.
- Doesn't coordinate with other professionals.
- Can't explain their systematic approach.
- Lacks experience with complex family situations.

Tax Professional

Key Questions to Ask:

1. "How do you plan for future tax years, not just current year filing?"

Look for: multi-year projections, strategic planning, proactive approach.

2. "Tell me about your coordination process with wealth managers and estate attorneys."

Look for: regular communication, integrated planning, shared documentation.

3. "How do you handle qualified rollovers and other complex transactions?"

Look for: experience with coding issues, error prevention, correction processes.

4. "What's your approach to estimated payments and cash flow planning?"

Look for: proactive planning, not reactive scrambling.

Must-Have Capabilities:
- Multi-year tax projection and planning
- Experience with high-net-worth complexity
- Coordination with financial advisors on money movements
- Proactive estimated payment planning
- Knowledge of business entity tax strategies
- Error correction experience (rollover miscoding, etc.)

Warning Signs:
- Only does annual filing, no forward planning.
- Doesn't communicate with other team members.
- Unfamiliar with complex transaction coding.
- Reactive approach to tax surprises.

Estate Planning Attorney

Key Questions to Ask:

1. "What percentage of your practice is dedicated to estate planning?"

Look for: 75%+ specialization, not a side practice.

2. "Do you have specialized estate planning drafting software?"

Look for: professional-grade tools, not generic forms.

3. "Tell me about a complex family situation you've handled recently."

Look for: experience with blended families, business owners, multi-generational planning.

4. "How do you coordinate with tax professionals and wealth managers?"

Look for: integrated planning approach, regular team communication.

Must-Have Capabilities:
- Must be an estate planning specialist
- Professional estate planning drafting software
- Experience with business succession planning
- Multi-generational wealth transfer strategies
- Asset protection integration knowledge
- Regular collaboration with financial team

Warning Signs:
- General practice attorney doing estate planning "on the side."
- No specialized drafting software.
- Limited experience with complex family structures.
- Works in isolation from other professionals.

Business Attorney

Key Questions to Ask:

1. "How much of your practice focuses on business law and entity structuring?"

Look for: dedicated business law specialization.

2. "Walk me through your approach to asset protection through business entities."

Look for: understanding of liability shields, proper structuring.

3. "How do you coordinate entity structures with estate and tax planning?"

Look for: Integrated approach, team collaboration.

4. "Tell me about your experience with business succession planning."

Look for: exit strategy experience, valuation understanding.

Must-Have Capabilities:
- Business entity specialization
- Asset protection through business structures

Must-Have Capabilities:
- Strategic risk assessment (not just product sales)
- Estate planning integration experience
- Business insurance and key person coverage
- Long-term care planning knowledge
- Advanced life insurance strategies (ILITs, etc.)
- Team coordination experience

Warning Signs:
- Product-focused salesperson mentality
- Doesn't coordinate with other professionals
- Limited high-net-worth experience
- Pushes products without strategic assessment

Red Flag Process

When to Remove a Team Member:
- Consistent communication problems
- Ego conflicts with other professionals
- Pushing their agenda over client goals
- Missing deadlines or deliverables
- Not following through on coordination commitments

Replacement Process:
- Document specific issues for reference.
- Identify replacement candidates using this checklist.
- Coordinate transition with remaining team members.
- Ensure no gaps in service during transition.

Final Team Validation

Your wealth team is ready when:
- Everyone knows their role and stays in their lane.
- Communication flows smoothly between all parties.

- Your goals drive all decisions, not professional agendas.
- No blind spots or gaps in coverage.
- Proactive planning happens regularly.
- You have confidence in the team's ability to protect and grow your wealth.

BUILD YOUR PERSONAL VAULT PLAN

Get a free 15 to 20 minute goals call to see if the VAULT system is the right fit for you and map out your first move toward bulletproof wealth.

SCHEDULE YOUR CALL

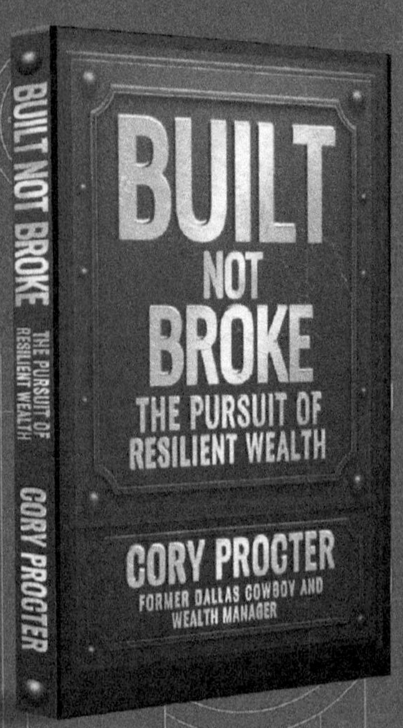

Scan the QR or visit
CORYPROCTER.COM

About the Author

Cory Procter is the Founder and CEO of Pro Capital Wealth Management (Pro Capital, LLC) a firm dedicated to helping entrepreneurs and business owners protect, grow, and transition their wealth with intention. Drawing on more than a decade of experience in wealth management and leadership, as well as a six-year career in the NFL, Cory brings a rare combination of discipline, strategy, and heart to every client relationship.

At Pro Capital, Cory and his team specialize in guiding growth-minded individuals with $1 million or more in investable assets. Their approach goes beyond investment advice, combining tax-smart planning, asset protection, exit strategy design, and multi-generational legacy planning. The firm's mission is simple: to protect the castles their clients have built and help their legacies endure for generations.

Cory's perspective on wealth is grounded in personal experience. He knows what it means to perform under pressure, make high-stakes decisions, and lead with purpose. These are the same skills he honed during his years as an offensive lineman with the Dallas Cowboys, Miami Dolphins, and Detroit Lions. That same mindset now drives his work with business owners navigating complex financial transitions.

In addition to leading Pro Capital, Cory is a dynamic speaker, podcast host, and board member of Majesty Outdoors, a nonprofit that mentors fatherless youth and single mothers. He is passionate about growth in every sense—financial, personal, and spiritual.

Cory lives in Trophy Club, Texas, with his wife Megan, an estate planning attorney, and their three children—Grace, Hank, and Faith. When he is not advising clients or speaking at events, he enjoys spending time outdoors with his family and helping others design legacies that last.

www.ingramcontent.com/pod-product-compliance
Lightning Source LLC
Chambersburg PA
CBHW071500140726
47997CB00005B/1798